SAMS
Teach Yourself

Office 97

Edited by Nancy Warner

in 10 Minutes

SAMS

A Division of Macmillan Computer Publishing
201 West 103rd St., Indianapolis, Indiana 46290 USA

Library of Congress Catalog Card Number: 98-84598

International Standard Book Number: 0-672-31321-9

00 99 98   8 7 6 5 4 3

Interpretation of the printing code: the rightmost double-digit number is the year of the book's first printing; the rightmost single-digit number is the number of the book's printing. For example, a printing code of 98-1 shows that this copy of the book was printed during the first printing of the book in 1998.

Screen reproductions in this book were created using Collage Plus from Inner Media, Inc., Hollis, NH.

Printed in the United States of America

Publisher John Pierce

Managing Editor Thomas F. Hayes

Acquisitions Editor Renee Wilmeth

Development Editor Nancy Warner

Book Designer Kim Scott

Cover Designer Dan Armstrong

Indexer Ginny Bess, Chris Wilcox

Production Team Angela Calvert, Mary Hunt

WE'D LIKE TO HEAR FROM YOU!

Sams has a long-standing reputation for high-quality books and products. To ensure your continued satisfaction, we also understand the importance of customer service and support.

TECH SUPPORT

If you need assistance with the information in this book, please access Macmillan Computer Publishing's online Knowledge Base at **http://www.superlibrary.com/general/support**. If you do not find the answer to your questions on our Web site, you may contact Macmillan Technical Support by phone at **317/581-3833** or via e-mail at **support@mcp.com**.

Also be sure to visit Macmillan's Web resource center for all the latest information, enhancements, errata, downloads, and more. It's located at **http://www.mcp.com/**.

ORDERS, CATALOGS, AND CUSTOMER SERVICE

To order other Sams or Macmillan Computer Publishing books, catalogs, or products, please contact our Customer Service Department at **800/858-7674** or fax us at **800/835-3202** (International Fax: 317/228-4400). Or visit our online bookstore at **http://www.mcp.com/**.

COMMENTS AND SUGGESTIONS

We want you to let us know what you like or dislike most about this book or other Sams products. Your comments will help us to continue publishing the best books available on computer topics in today's market.

Sams
201 West 103rd Street
Indianapolis, Indiana 46290 USA
Fax: 317/581-4663

Please be sure to include the book's title and author as well as your name and phone or fax number. We will carefully review your comments and share them with the author. Please note that due to the high volume of mail we receive, we may not be able to reply to every message.

CONTENTS

INTRODUCTION

If you need to learn Office 97 quickly, you've come to the right place. The *Sams' Teach Yourself Office 97 in 10 Minutes* is a guide to learning about the important features of this powerful software. Each lesson provides step-by-step instructions on a specific feature or function of Microsoft Office 97.

WHAT IS MICROSOFT OFFICE 97?

Microsoft Office consists of the following software packages:

- Word   Arguably the best Windows-based word processing program on the market. Word has features that enable you to create a one-page memo, a newsletter with graphics, or even a 500-page report.

- Excel   A powerful yet easy-to-maneuver spreadsheet program. Excel can be used to generate impressive financial statements, charts and graphs, and databases, and to share the information with other software packages.

- Access   A database program that is quickly becoming a leader in the industry because of its powerful capabilities and ease of use. Access is included only in the Professional edition of Office, not the standard version.

- PowerPoint   An easy-to-use presentation program that lets you create impressive slides and overheads or print-out presentations.

- Outlook   An electronic mail client, daily planner, calendar, and to-do list that helps you get the most out of your day through careful schedule management.

CONVENTIONS USED IN THIS BOOK

To help you move through the lessons easily, these conventions are used:

Onscreen text   Onscreen text appears in bold type.

Text you should type   Information you need to type appears in bold colored type.

Items you select   Commands, options, and icons you are to select and keys you are to press appear in colored type.

In telling you to choose menu commands, this book uses the format *menu title, menu command*. For example, the statement "choose File, Properties" means to "open the File menu and select the Properties command."

In addition to those conventions, this book uses the following icons to identify helpful information:

 Plain English   New or unfamiliar terms are defined in (you got it) "plain English."

 Timesaver Tips   Read these tips for ideas that cut corners and confusion.

 Panic Button   This icon identifies areas where new users often run into trouble; these tips offer practical solutions to those problems.

TRADEMARKS

All terms mentioned in this book that are known to be trademarks have been appropriately capitalized. Sams cannot attest to the accuracy of this information. Use of a term in this book should not be regarded as affecting the validity of any trademark or service mark.

ACKNOWLEDGMENTS

I would like to give a special thanks to Scott L. Warner, my better half, who helped develop the text and made me coffee at midnight (and it *still* tastes better than mine!).

A *big* thanks also to Renee Wilmeth for thinking of me—even after 2,000 miles—and all her support.

OFFICE 97 BASICS

In this lesson, you learn how to work with common Office 97 features as well as how to print.

STARTING A WINDOWS APPLICATION

A Windows application is a program designed to take advantage of the graphical user interface (GUI) built into Windows. A GUI provides a common interface between you and your programs that enables you to use the same procedures to execute commands in most compatible applications. That means that you can start (and exit) most Windows applications using the same procedures. If you are using a non-Windows (DOS) application through Windows, you need to consult that application's manual to learn how to start and exit.

To start a Windows-based application, follow these steps:

1. Click the Start button. The Start menu appears.

2. Point to Programs in the Start menu. The Programs menu appears.

3. Click the program folder that contains the program icon for the application you want to use.

4. Click the program icon for the application you want to start, and the application window appears. In this example, we are opening Windows Explorer (see Figure 1.1).

USING THE WINDOWS EXPLORER WINDOW

Figure 1.1 shows the Windows Explorer window. The All Folders pane (the left side of the screen) shows all the folders on the selected drive (in this case, drive C).

The left side of the Windows Explorer window contains the folder list, a graphical representation of the folders and subfolders on your system. (The folder list on your screen contains different folders from those shown in Figure 1.1.) You can see that drive C contains a folder named Windows, and the Windows folder has many subfolders, including one named All Users.

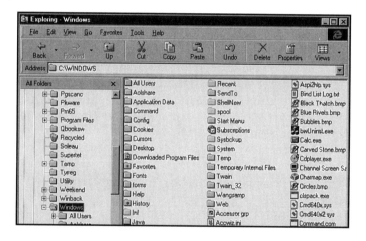

FIGURE 1.1   The Windows Explorer window, displaying the contents of the C drive.

 Folders and Subfolders   The folder that leads to all other folders is the main folder. In Figure 1.1, the main folder is C:. Any folder can have a subfolder. Subfolders are like file folders within file folders; they help you organize your files.

The right side of the window contains a list of the files in the folder that's currently highlighted in the folder list. Notice that the folder icon next to the Windows folder (the highlighted folder) appears as an open folder. In this figure, the files and folders in the Windows (root directory) folder are listed in the right pane of the Windows Explorer window.

The status bar shows the number of objects in the window, the disk space those objects occupy, and the amount of remaining empty disk space.

SEARCHING FOR A FILE

As you create more files, the capability to find a specific file becomes more critical. You can search for either a single file or a group of files with similar names by using the Tools, Find command. To search for a group of files, use the asterisk wild card (*) with a partial filename to narrow the search. You also can perform a partial name search without wild cards, search by last modification date, save complex searches, and do a full text search. (Table 1.1 shows some search examples and their potential results.)

 Wild Cards When you're not sure of the filename you want to find, you can use the asterisk wild card (*) to replace multiple characters in the filename or the question mark wild card (?) to replace one character in the filename.

TABLE 1.1   EXAMPLES AND THEIR RESULTS

CHARACTERS ENTERED FOR SEARCH	SAMPLE SEARCH RESULTS
mem?.doc	mem1.doc, mem2.doc, memo.doc
mem1.doc	mem1.doc
mem*.doc	mem1.doc, mem2.doc, mem10.doc, memos.doc

continued

TABLE 1.1 CONTINUED

CHARACTERS ENTERED FOR SEARCH	SAMPLE SEARCH RESULTS
c*.exe	calc.exe, calendar.exe
*.exe	calc.exe, calendar.exe, notepad.exe
c*.*	calc.exe, calendar.exe, class.doc

To search for a file, follow these steps:

1. Click the Start button, select Find, and select Files or Folders. The Find dialog box appears.

2. In the Named text box, enter the characters you want to find, using wild cards to identify unknown characters (see Figure 1.2).

3. If you want to search the entire drive, choose C: in the Look In text box (if it's not already there) and make sure the Include Subfolders check box is selected.

   If you want to search only the main folder, make sure the Include Subfolders check box is not selected.

   If you want to search a specific folder, click the Browse button and select a folder from the folders list.

4. If you want to search for a file according to its last modification date, select the Date Modified tab and select the date options you want.

5. If you want to search for a certain type of file, select the Advanced tab and choose a file type in the Of Type drop-down list box.

6. When you finish setting options, click the Find Now button to begin the search. The search results window appears under the Find dialog box, showing the files that were found (see Figure 1.3).

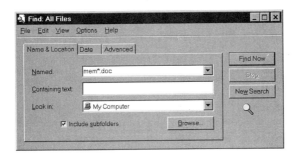

FIGURE 1.2   A completed Find dialog box.

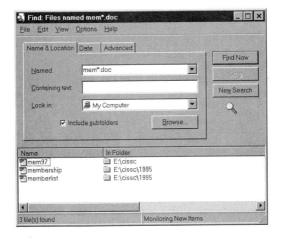

FIGURE 1.3   The search results appear below the Find settings.

PRINTING FROM A WINDOWS APPLICATION

To print from any Windows application, choose File, Print. A Print dialog box appears, asking you to specify a number of options. The options available depend on the application. When you click OK in this dialog box, the application hands off the font and file information to the Printers folder. This enables you to continue working in your application while your job is printing.

The Printers folder acts as the middleman between your printer and the application from which you are printing.

SELECTING PRINT SETTINGS

To specify print settings before you print a file, open the File menu and choose Page Setup. You'll see the Page Setup dialog box. The following list outlines the common page setup settings (each application will have slightly different tab options):

Orientation   Select Portrait to print across the short edge of a page; select Landscape to print across the long edge of a page. (Landscape makes the page wider than it is tall.)

Scaling   You can reduce and enlarge your page or force it to fit within a specific page size.

Paper Size   This is 8 1/2 by 11 inches by default, but you can choose a different size from the list.

Print Quality   You can print in draft quality to print quickly and save wear and tear on your printer, or you can print in high quality for a final copy. Print quality is measured in dpi (dots per inch); the higher the number, the better the print.

First Page Number   You can set the starting page number to something other than 1. The Auto option (default) sets the starting page number to 1 if it is the first page in the print job, or to set the first page number at the next sequential number if it is not the first page in the print job.

Top, Bottom, Left, Right   You can adjust the size of the top, bottom, left, and right margins.

Header, Footer   You can specify how far you want a Header or Footer printed from the edge of the page.

Center on Page   You can center the information on a page between the left and right margins (Horizontally) and between the top and bottom margins (Vertically).

Header, Footer   You can add a header (such as a title) that repeats at the top of each page, or a footer (such as page numbers) that repeats at the bottom of each page.

Custom Header, Custom Footer   You can use the Custom Header or Custom Footer button to create headers and footers that insert the time, date, and filename.

When you finish entering your settings, click the OK button.

USING PRINT PREVIEW

The Print Preview feature lets you view your document exactly as it will be printed. Although Page Layout view also displays your document in its final form, Print Preview offers some additional features that you may find useful. To use Print Preview, select File, Print Preview or click the Print Preview button on the Standard toolbar.

These guidelines outline your available options in the Preview window:

- Press Page Up or Page Down or use the vertical scroll bar to view other pages.

- Click the Multiple Pages button and drag over the page icons to preview more than one page at once. Click the One Page button to preview a single page.

- Click the Zoom Control drop-down arrow and select a magnification to preview the document at different magnifications.

- Click the View Ruler button to display the Ruler. You can then use the Ruler to set page margins and indents.

- Click the Magnifier button and click in the document to enlarge that part of the document.

- Click the Shrink To Fit button to prevent a small amount of text from spilling onto the document's last page.

- Click the Print button to print the document. Click again to return to the original view.

- Click Close or press Esc to end Print Preview display.

EXITING WINDOWS APPLICATIONS

Before you exit an application, be sure to save and close any documents on which you have worked in that application (using the File, Save and File, Close commands).

After you have saved and closed all document files, you can exit a Windows application by using any of the following four methods:

- To exit an application using its Control-menu icon (the icon in the upper-left corner of the application window), double-click the Control-menu icon.

- To exit an application using its Close button, click the Close button (the button with an X at the right end of the application's title bar).

- To exit an application using the menus, choose File, Exit.

- The quickest way to exit is to use the shortcut key. Press Alt+F4.

In this lesson, you learned how to work with common Office 97 features as well as how to print.

FORMATTING DOCUMENTS

LESSON

In this lesson, you learn how to work with the different formatting features in Word.

SELECTING A FONT

Word offers you a huge assortment of fonts to use in your documents. Each font has a specific typeface, which determines the appearance of the characters. Typefaces are identified by names such as Arial, Courier, and Times New Roman. Each font also has many sizes, which are specified in points. There are 72 points in an inch, so a 36-point font would have its largest characters $1/2$ inch tall. Most documents use font sizes in the 8- to 14-point range, but larger and smaller sizes are available for headings and other special needs.

You can change the font of text that already has been typed by first selecting the text. To specify the font for text you are about to type, move the cursor to the desired location. Then follow these steps to choose a font for the selected text or the text you're about to type:

1. Click Format, Font to open the Font dialog box shown in Figure 2.1.

2. The Font text box displays the name of the current font. Scroll through the Font list box and select a new font name.

3. The Size text box displays the current font size. Select a new size from the Size list box or type a number in the text box. The Preview box shows the appearance of the selected font. Click OK to enter your settings.

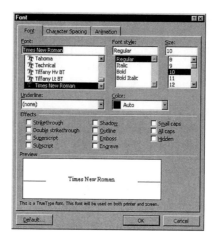

FIGURE 2.1   The Font dialog box.

You can quickly select a font name and size using the Formatting toolbar. The Font list box and the Font Size list box display the name and size of the current font. You can change the font by clicking the drop-down arrow of either list and making a selection. Note that in the Font list, the fonts you have used recently appear at the top.

 Quick Select   If you want to change the font for a whole document, remember that you can select the entire document by pressing Ctrl+A.

USING BOLDFACE, ITALICS, AND UNDERLINING

You can apply bold, italics, or underlining to any of Word's fonts. You can also use two or three of these effects in combination. As you can with other formatting, you can apply these effects to existing text by first selecting the text, or you can apply them to text you are about to type.

The quickest way to assign boldface, italics, or underlining is with the buttons on the Formatting toolbar. Click a button to turn the corresponding attribute on; click it again to turn it off. When the cursor is at a location where one of these attributes is turned on, the corresponding toolbar button appears to be pressed in.

APPLYING SPECIAL FONT EFFECTS

Word has a number of special font effects that you can use. These include superscript and subscript, strikethrough, and several graphics effects (such as shadow and outline). You can also specify that text be hidden, which means it will not display on-screen or be printed.

To assign special font effects to selected text or text you are about to type, open the Font dialog box. In the Effects area, select the effects you want. To turn on an effect, click to place an X in the check box. To turn off an effect, click to remove the X from the check box. The Preview box shows you what the font will look like with the selected effects. When you're satisfied with your settings, click OK.

DISPLAYING BORDERS

Word's Borders command lets you improve the appearance of your documents by displaying borders around selected text. Figure 2.2 shows examples of the use of borders (and it illustrates shading.

You can apply a border to selected text or to individual paragraphs. To put a border around text, select the text. For a paragraph, place the cursor anywhere in the paragraph. The quickest way to apply a border is to use the Border button on the Formatting toolbar. Click the Border drop-down arrow to view a palette of available border settings, and then click the desired border diagram. Click the No Borders diagram to remove borders.

If you need more control over the appearance of your borders, you must use the Borders and Shading dialog box (see Figure 2.3).

To open this dialog box, click Format, Borders And Shading, and then click the Borders tab if necessary.

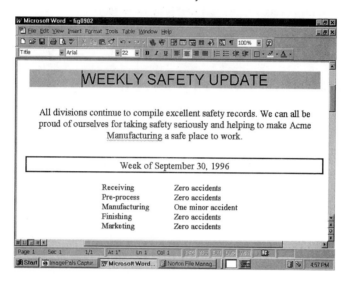

FIGURE 2.2   A document with borders and shading.

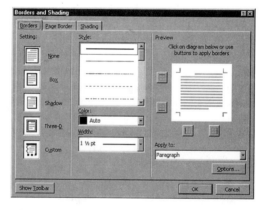

FIGURE 2.3   The Borders tab of the Borders and Shading dialog box.

The normal border settings apply the same line style (solid, dotted, and so on) to all four sides of the border box, though you can create a custom border that combines different styles.

You can also place borders around entire pages in your document. To do so, click the Page Border tab of the Borders And Shading dialog box. This tab looks and operates just as the Borders tab does in terms of specifying the border's appearance. The only difference is specifying where the border will be applied, which is done with the options in the Apply To list.

Applying Shading

You can use shading to display a background color under text (such as black text on a light gray background). Figure 2.4 shows an example of shading. You can apply shading to selected text or to individual paragraphs. Shading can be made up of a fill color, a pattern color, or a combination of both.

Here's how to apply shading:

1. Select the text to be shaded, or position the cursor anywhere in the paragraph to shade an entire paragraph.

2. Click Format, Borders And Shading to open the Borders and Shading dialog box. If necessary, click the Shading tab (see Figure 2.4).

3. To use a fill color, select it from the palette in the Fill area of the dialog box. To use only a pattern color, click the None button.

4. To use a pattern color, select its style and color from the lists in the Patterns section of the dialog box. To use only a fill color, select the Clear style. You can view the appearance of the selected settings in the Preview area of the dialog box.

5. If you selected text before opening the dialog box, use the Apply To list to specify whether the fill should apply to the selected text or the current paragraph. Click OK.

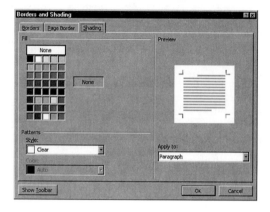

FIGURE 2.4   The Shading tab of the Borders and Shading dialog box.

UTILIZING INDENTATION

The distance between your text and the left and right edges of the page is controlled by two things: the left and right page margins and the text indentation. Margins are usually changed only for entire documents or large sections of a document. For smaller sections of text, such as individual lines and paragraphs, you will use indentation.

The easiest way to set indents is by using the Ruler and your mouse. To display the Ruler (or hide it), click View, Ruler. The numbers on the Ruler indicate the space from the left margin in inches. Figure 2.5 shows the Ruler and identifies the various elements you use to set indents. In addition, the sample text in the figure illustrates the various indent options.

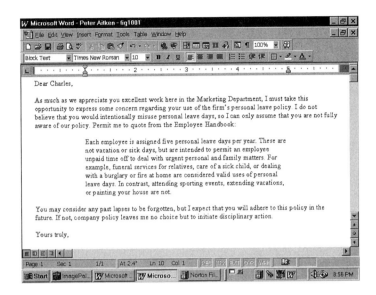

FIGURE 2.5   Use the Ruler to set text indentation. The second paragraph is indented one inch from both the right and left margins.

To set indentation for one paragraph, position the cursor anywhere in the paragraph. For more than one paragraph, select those paragraphs. (Otherwise, the new indents will apply only to new paragraphs that you type from the insertion point forward.) Then drag the indent markers on the Ruler to the desired positions. As you drag, a dotted vertical line appears, stretching down through the document to show the new indent's location. Use these guidelines when setting paragraph indentation:

- To change the indent of the first line of a paragraph, drag the First Line Indent marker to the desired position.

- To change the indent of all lines of a paragraph except the first one, drag the Other Lines Indent marker to the desired position (this is called a hanging indent).

- To change the indent of all lines of a paragraph, drag the All Lines Indent marker to the desired position.

- To change the indent of the right edge of the paragraph, drag the Right Indent marker to the desired position.

You also can quickly increase or decrease the left indent for the current paragraph in ¹/₂-inch increments by clicking the Increase Indent or Decrease Indent buttons on the Formatting toolbar. And undoubtedly, the quickest way to indent the first line of a paragraph is to position the cursor at the start of the line and press Tab.

SETTING TEXT JUSTIFICATION

Justification, sometimes called alignment, refers to the manner in which the left and right ends of lines of text are aligned.

Figure 2.6 illustrates the justification options. To change the justification for one or more paragraphs, first select the paragraphs to change. Then click one of the justification buttons on the Formatting toolbar. The toolbar button corresponding to the current paragraph's justification setting appears to be pressed in.

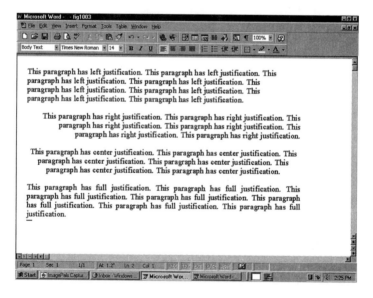

FIGURE 2.6   Click these buttons to set text justification.

WORKING WITH TABS

Tabs provide a way for you to control the indentation and vertical alignment of text in your document. When you press the Tab key, Word inserts a tab in the document and moves the cursor (and any text to the right of it) to the next tab stop. By default, Word has tab stops at 0.5-inch intervals across the width of the page. You can modify the location of tab stops and control the way text aligns at a tab stop.

Figure 2.7 illustrates the effects of the four tab alignment options and shows the four markers that appear on the Ruler to indicate the position of tab stops.

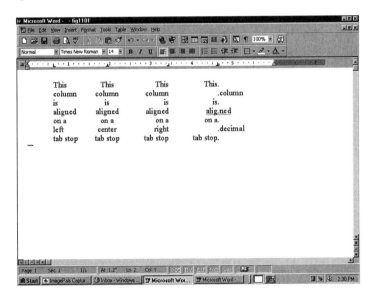

FIGURE 2.7   The four tab stop alignment options.

CHANGING THE DEFAULT TAB STOPS

Default tab stops affect all paragraphs for which you have not set custom tab stops (covered in the next section). You cannot delete the default tab stops, but you can change the spacing between them. The default tab stop spacing affects the entire document. Here are the steps to follow:

1. Click Format, Tabs to display the Tabs dialog box, shown in Figure 2.8.

2. In the Default Tab Stops box, click the increment arrows to increase or decrease the spacing between default tab stops. Click OK.

 Good-Bye Tab   To effectively *delete* the default tab stops, set the spacing between them to a value larger than the page width.

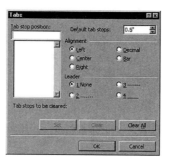

FIGURE 2.8   The Tabs dialog box.

CREATING CUSTOM TAB STOPS

If the default tab stops are not suited to your needs, you can add custom tab stops. The number, spacing, and type of custom tab stops is totally up to you. Use these steps to set custom tab stops:

1. Select the paragraphs that will have custom tabs. If no text is selected, the new tabs will affect the paragraph containing the cursor and new text you type.

2. Click the tab symbol at the left end of the Ruler until it displays the marker for the type of tab you want to insert (refer to Figure 2.9).

3. Point at the approximate tab stop location on the Ruler, and press and hold the left mouse button. A dashed vertical line extends down through the document to show the tab stop position relative to your text.

4. Move the mouse left or right until the tab stop is at the desired location and release the mouse button.

 No Ruler?   If your Ruler is not displayed, click View, Ruler or position the mouse pointer near the top edge of the work area for a few seconds.

When you add a custom tab stop, all the default tab stops to the left are temporarily inactivated. This ensures that the custom tab stop will take precedence. If custom tab stops have been defined for the current paragraph, the custom tabs are displayed on the Ruler; otherwise, the default tab stops are displayed.

MOVING AND DELETING CUSTOM TAB STOPS

To move a custom tab stop to a new position, point at the tab stop marker on the Ruler and press and hold the left mouse button. Drag the tab stop to the new position and then release the mouse button.

To delete a custom tab stop, follow the same steps, but instead of dragging the tab stop to a new position, drag the tab stop marker off the Ruler and release the mouse button.

CHANGING LINE SPACING

Line spacing controls the amount of vertical space between lines of text. Different spacing is appropriate for different kinds of documents. If you want to print your document on as few pages as possible, use single line spacing to position lines close together. In contrast, a document that will later be edited by hand should be printed with wide line spacing to provide space for the editor to write comments.

Word offers a variety of line spacing options. If you change line spacing, it affects the selected text; if there is no text selected, it affects the current paragraph and text you type at the insertion point.

Follow these steps to change line spacing:

1. Click Format, Paragraph to open the Paragraph dialog box. If necessary, click the Indents And Spacing tab (see Figure 2.9).

2. Click the Line Spacing drop-down arrow and select the desired spacing option from the list. The Single, 1.5 Lines, and Double settings are self-explanatory. Test some of the other options like Exactly, At Least, and Multiple.

3. To add spacing before the first line or after the last line of the paragraph, enter the desired space (in points), or click the arrows in the Before and After text boxes. Click OK.

FIGURE 2.9   The Paragraph dialog box with the Indents and Spacing options displayed.

CONTROLLING LINE BREAKS

The word wrap feature automatically breaks each line in a paragraph when it reaches the right margin. Word offers a couple of methods for controlling the way lines break. You can prevent a line break from occurring between two specific words to ensure that the words always remain together on the same line. These methods can be particularly useful when you modify indents and justification because this often changes where individual lines break.

Word's default is to break lines as needed at spaces or hyphens. To prevent a line break, you must insert a nonbreaking space or a nonbreaking hyphen instead. To insert a nonbreaking hyphen, press Ctrl+Shift+- (hyphen). To insert a nonbreaking space, press Ctrl+Shift+Spacebar.

You also can use an optional hyphen to specify where a word can be broken, if necessary. This is useful with long words that may fall at the end of the line; if word wrap moves the long word to the next line, there will be an unsightly gap at the end of the previous line. An optional hyphen remains hidden unless the word extends past the right margin. Then the hyphen appears, and only the part of the word after the hyphen wraps to the new line. To insert an optional hyphen, press Ctrl+- (hyphen).

Finally, you can insert a line break without starting a new paragraph by pressing Shift+Enter.

USING SECTION BREAKS

Word gives you the option of breaking you document into two or more sections, each of which can have its own page formatting. Word offers three types of section breaks. They have the same effect in terms of controlling page layout, but differ as to where the text that comes after the break is placed:

- Next Page   The new section begins at the top of the next page.
- Continuous   The new section begins on the same page as the preceding section.
- Odd Page or Even Page   The new section begins on the next even- or odd-numbered page.

In Normal view, Word marks the location of section breaks by displaying a double horizontal line with the label Section Break followed by the type of break. These markers do not appear in page Layout view or in printouts.

To insert a section break, click Insert, Break to open the Break dialog box. Select the desired type of section break (as described in the previous list) and click OK.

A section break mark is just like any character in your document. To delete a section break, place the cursor right before it and press Delete, or place the cursor right after it and press Backspace.

INSERTING MANUAL PAGE BREAKS

When text reaches the bottom margin of a page, Word automatically starts a new page and continues the text at the top of that page. However, you can manually insert page breaks to start a new page at any desired location.

The quickest way to enter a new page break is by pressing Ctrl+Enter. To start a new line without starting a new paragraph, press Shift+Enter.

A page break appears in the document as a single horizontal line. Like section break markers, page break markers do not appear in Page Layout view or in printouts. To delete a page break, move the cursor to the line containing the break and press Delete.

In this lesson, you learned how to use work with the different formatting features in Word.

PROOFREADING DOCUMENTS

In this lesson, you learn how to find and replace text, use the spelling checker, the thesaurus, and check your grammar in Word documents.

FINDING AND REPLACING TEXT IN WORD

With Word's Find and Replace features, you can locate certain text and replace it with new text. Word can search through your document to find occurrences of specific text. The default is to search the entire document; that's what it does unless you select some text before you issue the command. If you select text first, it searches only the selected text. To find text, follow these steps:

1. Click Edit, Find or press Ctrl+F. The Find and Replace dialog box appears (see Figure 3.1).

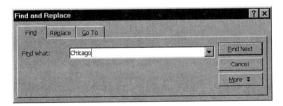

FIGURE 3.1 The Find tab in the Find and Replace dialog box.

2. In the Find What text box, enter the text for which you want to search. The text you enter is called the search template.

3. Click Find Next. Word looks through the document for text that matches the search template. If it finds matching

text, it highlights it in the document and stops; the Find dialog box remains on-screen.

4. Click Find Next to continue the search for other instances of the search template. Or, press Esc to close the dialog box and return to the document. The found text remains selected.

When Word finishes searching the entire document, it displays one of two messages. It will inform you that the search template cannot be found, or it will let you know the search is complete.

 Find or Replace   You can access the Find dialog box from the Replace dialog box (and vice versa) by clicking the corresponding tab.

Word's Replace command lets you search for instances of text and replace them with new text. This can be very helpful if, for example, you misspelled the same word multiple times in the same document. To find and replace text, follow these steps:

1. Click Edit, Replace or press Ctrl+H. The Find and Replace dialog box appears (see Figure 3.2).

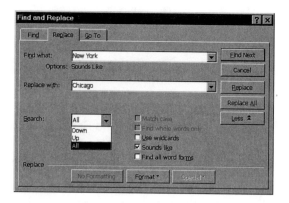

FIGURE 3.2   The Replace tab in the Find and Replace dialog box.

Recovery! If you make a mistake replacing text, you can recover by clicking **Edit**, **Undo Replace**.

2. In the Find What text box, enter the text you want to replace.

3. In the Replace With text box, enter the replacement text.

4. (Optional) Click the More button and specify search options as explained in the previous section.

5. Click Find Next to locate and highlight the first instance of the target text.

6. For each occurrence Word finds, respond using one of these buttons:

   • Click Replace to replace the highlighted instance of the target text and then locate the next instance of it.

   • Click Find Next to leave the highlighted instance of the target text unchanged and to locate the next instance.

   • Click Replace All to replace all instances of the target text in the entire document.

 Deleting Text To delete the target text, follow the previous steps but leave the Replace With text box empty.

USING SEARCH OPTIONS IN WORD

The default Find operation locates the search template you specify without regard to the case of letters or whether it's a whole word or part of a word. For example, if you enter the search template "the," Word will find "the," "THE," "mother," and so on. You can refine your search by using Word's search options. To do so, click the More button in the Find and Replace dialog box. The dialog box expands to offer additional options (see Figure 3.3).

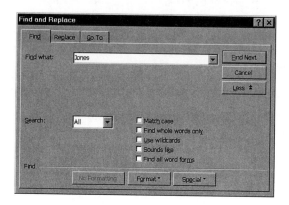

FIGURE 3.3   Setting options for the Find command.

You can choose from the following options:

- Match Case   Requires an exact match for uppercase and lowercase letters. By selecting this check box, "The" will match only "The" and not "the" or "THE."

- Find Whole Words Only   This will match whole words only. If you select this check box, "the" will match only "the"—not "mother," "these," and so on.

- Use Wildcards   Permits the use of the * and ? wildcards in the search template. The * wildcard stands in for any sequence of 0 or more unknown characters; the ? wildcard stands in for any single unknown character. Thus the template "th?n" would match "thin" and "then" but not "thrown" or "thn." And the template "th*n" would match "thin," "thn," "thrown," and so on.

- Sounds Like   Finds words that sound similar to the template. If you select this check box, for example, "their" will match "there."

- Find All Word Forms   Locates alternate forms of the search template. For example, "sit" will match not only "sit" but also "sat" and "sitting." This check box is not available if you select the Use Wildcards check box.

If you can't find text that you're sure is in the document, check the spelling of the search template and make sure unwanted search options are not enabled.

USING THE SPELLING CHECKER IN WORD

Word's spelling checker lets you verify and correct the spelling of words in your documents. Words are checked against a standard dictionary and unknown words are flagged. You can then ignore the word, correct it, or add it to the dictionary.

To check spelling in a portion of a document, select the text to check. Otherwise Word will check the entire document starting at the location of the cursor. If you want to check starting at the beginning of the document, move the insertion point to the start of the document by pressing Ctrl+Home. Then follow these steps:

1. Select Tools, Spelling And Grammar, or press F7, or click the Spelling And Grammar button on the Standard toolbar. The Spelling And Grammar dialog box appears (see Figure 3.4). If you want to check spelling only, deselect the Check Grammar check box. The remainder of these steps assume that you are only checking spelling.

2. When Word locates a word in the document that is not in the dictionary, it displays the word and its surrounding text in the Not in Dictionary list box with the word highlighted in red. In Figure 3.4, for example, the word checker is highlighted. Suggested replacements for the word appear in the Suggestions list box (if Word has no suggestions, this box will be empty). For each word that Word stops on, take action in one of these ways:

   - To correct the word manually, edit it in the Not In Dictionary list box and click Change.

- To use one of the suggested replacements, highlight the desired replacement word in the Suggestions list box and click Change.

- To replace all instances of the word in the document with either the manual corrections you made or the word selected in the Suggestions box, click Change All.

- To ignore this instance of the word, click Ignore.

- To ignore this and all other instances of the word in the document, click Ignore All.

- To add the word to the dictionary, click Add.

3. Repeat as needed. When the entire document has been checked, Word displays a message to that effect. (Or, you can click Cancel at any time to end spell checking early.)

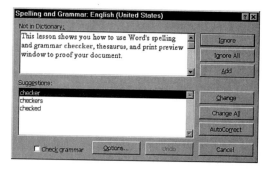

FIGURE 3.4 Checking spelling in the Spelling and Grammar dialog box.

CHECKING YOUR GRAMMAR IN WORD

Word can check the grammar of the text in your document, flagging possible problems so that you can correct them if needed. Here are the steps required to run the grammar checker:

1. Select Tools, Spelling And Grammar, or press F7, or click the Spelling And Grammar button on the toolbar. The

Spelling and Grammar dialog box appears (refer to Figure 3.4). Make sure the Check Grammar check box is selected.

2. When Word locates a word or phrase with a suspected grammatical error, it displays the word or phrase and its surrounding text in the dialog box with the word highlighted in green and a description of the suspected problem above the text. In Figure 3.5, for example, the word wants is highlighted and the problem Subject-Verb Agreement appears. Suggested fixes, if any, are listed in the Suggestions list box. For each potential mistake that Word stops on, take action in one of these ways:

   - To manually correct the error, edit the text and click Change.

   - To use one of the suggested replacements, select it in the Suggestions list box and click Change.

   - To ignore this instance of the problem, click Ignore.

   - To ignore this instance and all other instances of the problem in the document, click Ignore All.

3. Word will check spelling at the same time it is checking grammar. Deal with spelling errors as explained earlier in this lesson.

4. Repeat as needed. When the entire document has been checked, Word displays a message to that effect. (Or, you can click Close at any time to end grammar checking early.)

 Don't Rely on Word Word's grammar checker is a useful tool, but don't rely on it to catch everything. It is no substitute for careful writing and editing.

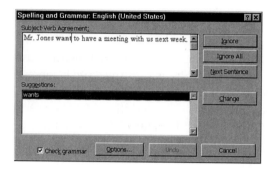

FIGURE 3.5   Checking grammar in the Spelling and Grammar dialog box.

USING THE THESAURUS IN WORD

A thesaurus provides you with synonyms and antonyms for words in your document. Using the thesaurus can help you avoid repetition in your writing (and improve your vocabulary).

To use the thesaurus, complete the following steps:

1. Place the insertion point on the word of interest in your document.

2. Press Shift+F7 or select Tools, Thesaurus. The Thesaurus dialog box opens (see Figure 3.6). This dialog box has several components:

   • The Looked Up list box displays the word of interest.

   • The Meanings list box lists alternate meanings for the word. If the word is not found, Word displays an Alphabetical List box instead; this list contains a list of words with spellings similar to the selected word.

   • If the thesaurus finds one or more meanings for the word, the dialog box displays the Replace with Synonym list showing synonyms for the currently highlighted meaning of the word. If meanings are not found, the dialog box displays a Replace with Related Word list.

3. While the Thesaurus dialog box is displayed, take one of these actions:

- To find synonyms for the highlighted word in the Replace With Synonym list or the Replace With Related Words list (depending on which one is displayed), click Look Up.

- To find synonyms for a word in the Meanings list, select the word and then click Look Up.

- For some words, the thesaurus displays the term Antonyms in the Meanings list. To display antonyms for the selected word, highlight the term Antonyms and then click Look Up.

4. To replace the word in the document with the highlighted word in the Replace With Synonym list or the Replace With Related Word list, click Replace.

5. To close the thesaurus without making any changes to the document, click Cancel.

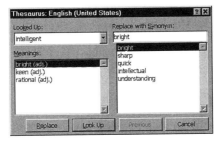

FIGURE 3.6   The Thesaurus dialog box.

In this lesson, you learned how to find and replace text, use the spelling checker, the thesaurus, and check your grammar in Word documents.

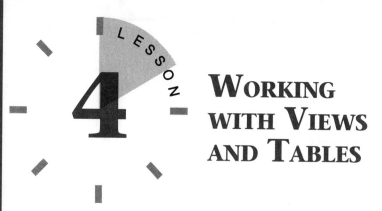

WORKING WITH VIEWS AND TABLES

In this lesson, you learn how to control the Word screen display to suit your working style, how to add tables to your document, and how to edit and format tables.

DOCUMENT DISPLAY OPTIONS

Word offers several ways to display your document. Each of these views is designed to make certain editing tasks easier. The available views include:

- Normal   Best for general editing tasks.

- Page Layout   Ideal for working with formatting and page layout.

- Online Layout   Optimized for viewing onscreen.

- Outline   Designed for working with outlines.

- Master Document   Designed for managing large, multi-part projects.

The view you use has no effect on the contents of your document or on the way it will look when printed. They affect only the way the document appears onscreen.

NORMAL VIEW

Normal view is suitable for most editing tasks; it is the view you will probably use most often. This is Word's default view. All special formatting is visible onscreen, including different font sizes, italic, boldface, and other enhancements. The screen display of your document is essentially identical to how the document will appear when printed. However, Word does not display certain aspects of the page layout, which makes it easier and quicker for you to edit. For example, you do not see headers and footers or multiple columns.

To select Normal view, click View, Normal or click the Normal View button at the left end of the horizontal scroll bar. Figure 4.1 shows a document in Normal view.

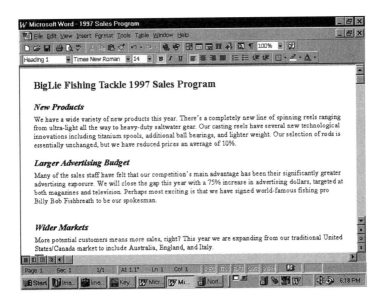

FIGURE 4.1   A document displayed in Normal view.

PAGE LAYOUT VIEW

Page Layout view displays your document exactly as it will print. Headers, footers, and all other details of the page layout appear onscreen. You can edit in Page Layout view; it's ideal for fine-tuning the details of page composition. Be aware, however, that the additional computer processing required makes display changes relatively slow in Page Layout view, particularly when you have a complex page layout.

Sneak Preview Use Page Layout view to see what your printed document will look like before you actually print. The Print Preview feature (File, Print Preview) is preferred for previewing entire pages.

Click View, Page Layout (or click the Page Layout View button) to switch to Page Layout view. Figure 4.2 shows a sample document in Page Layout view.

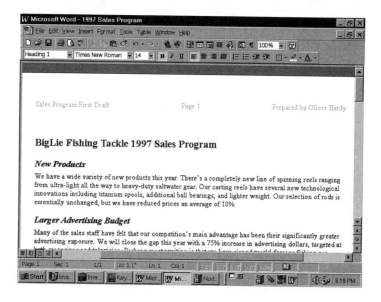

FIGURE 4.2 A document in Page Layout view displays the header.

ONLINE LAYOUT VIEW

Online Layout view is optimal for reading and editing a document onscreen. Legibility is increased by using larger fonts; displaying shorter lines of text; hiding headers, footers, and similar elements; and basing the layout on the screen as opposed to the printed page. Also, the document map is displayed on the left side of the screen (the document map is covered later in this lesson). The screen display will not match the final printed appearance. Online Layout view is ideal for editing the document text, but is not suited for working with page layout or graphics.

 Content Editing Use   Online Layout view when editing the document's contents, not the appearance.

Click View, Online Layout (or click the Online Layout View button) to switch to Online Layout view.

When you're in Online Layout view, the horizontal scroll bar and its View buttons are hidden. You must use the View menu commands to switch to a different view. Figure 4.3 shows a document in Online Layout view.

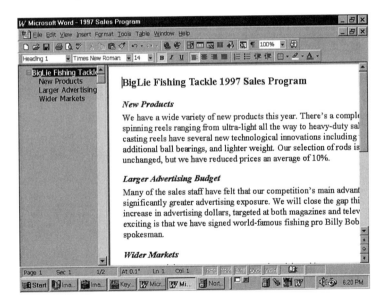

FIGURE 4.3   A document displayed in Online Layout view.

OUTLINE VIEW

Use Outline view to create outlines and to examine the structure of a document. Figure 4.4 shows a document in Outline view. In this view, you can choose to view only your document headings, thus hiding all subordinate text. You can quickly promote, demote, or move document headings along with subordinate text to a new location. For this view to be useful, you need to assign heading styles to the document headings, a technique you learn about in Lesson 5, "Working with Styles and Templates."

Click View, Outline to switch to Outline view, or click the Outline View button at the left end of the horizontal scroll bar.

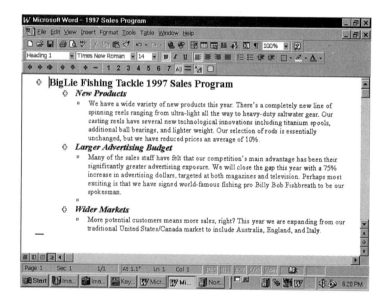

FIGURE 4.4   A document displayed in Outline view.

SPLITTING THE SCREEN

Word lets you split the work area into two panels, one above the other, so you can view different parts of one document at the same time. Each panel scrolls independently and has its own scroll bars. Figure 4.5 shows a document displayed on a split screen. Editing changes that you make in either panel affect the document. These steps walk you through splitting the screen:

1. Select Window, Split or press Ctrl+Alt+S. Word displays a horizontal split line across the middle of the work area.

2. To accept two equal size panes, click with the left mouse button or press Enter. To create different size panes, move the mouse until the split line is in the desired location, and then click or press Enter.

When working with a split screen, you move the editing cursor from one pane to the other by clicking with the mouse. To change the pane sizes, point at the split line and drag it to the new location. To remove the split and return to regular view, drag the split line to either the top or the bottom of the work area, or select Windows, Remove Split.

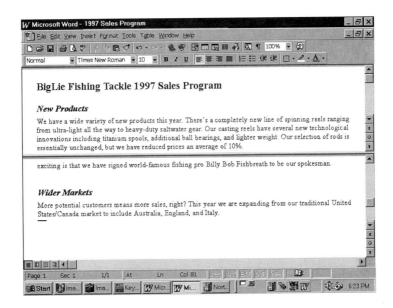

FIGURE 4.5 Viewing a document in split screen view.

Quick Split You can quickly split the screen by dragging the splitter bar, located just above the up arrow on the vertical toolbar.

INSERTING A TABLE

A table lets you organize information in a row and column format. Each entry in a table, called a *cell*, is independent of all other entries. You can have almost any number of rows and columns in a table. You also have a great deal of control over the size and formatting of each cell. A table cell can contain text, graphics, and just about anything that a Word document can contain. The one exception is that a table cannot contain another table.

To insert a new empty table at any location within your document, follow these steps:

1. Move the cursor to the document location where you want the table.

2. Select Table, Insert Table. The Insert Table dialog box appears (see Figure 4.6).

3. In the Number of Columns and Number of Rows text boxes, click the arrows or enter the number of rows and columns the table should have. (You can adjust these numbers later.)

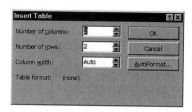

FIGURE 4.6   The Insert Table dialog box.

4. To apply one of Word's automatic table formats to the table, click the AutoFormat button, select the desired format, and click OK.

5. In the Column Width text box, select the desired width for each column (in inches). Select Auto in this box to have the page width evenly divided among the specified number of columns. Click OK. Word creates a blank table with the cursor in the first cell.

Quick Tables   To quickly insert a table, click the Insert Table button on the Standard toolbar and drag over the desired number of rows and columns.

After you create a table and enter some information, you can edit its contents and format its appearance to suit your needs. The following sections explain common editing and formatting tasks you might want to perform.

DELETING AND INSERTING CELLS, ROWS, AND COLUMNS

You can clear individual cells in a table, erasing their contents and leaving the cells blank. To clear the contents of a cell, simply select the cell and press Delete.

Fast Select!   You can select the text in the cell or the entire cell itself. To select an entire cell, click in the left margin of the cell, between the text and the cell border. The mouse pointer changes to an arrow when it's in this area.

You can also remove entire rows and columns. When you do so, columns to the right or rows below move to fill in for the deleted row or column. To completely remove a row or column from the table, follow these steps:

1. Move the cursor to any cell in the row or column to be deleted.

2. Select Table, Delete Cells. The Delete Cells dialog box appears (see Figure 4.7).

3. Select Delete Entire Row or Delete Entire Column. Click OK, and Word deletes the row or column.

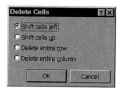

FIGURE 4.7   The Delete Cells dialog box.

Follow these steps to insert a single row or column into a table:

1. Move the cursor to a cell to the right of where you want the new column or below where you want the new row.

2. Select Table, Insert Columns to insert a new blank column to the left of the selected column. Select Table, Insert Rows to insert a new blank row above the selected row.

Use these steps to insert more than one row or column into a table:

1. Select cells that span the number of rows or columns you want to insert. For example, to insert three new rows between rows 2 and 3, select cells in rows 3, 4, and 5 (in any column). To select several cells, drag across them or select one and then hold down Shift and use the arrow keys to extend the selections.

2. Select Table, Select Row (if inserting rows) or Table, Select Column (if inserting columns).

3. Select Table, Insert Rows or Table, Insert Columns as appropriate.

 Add a Row To insert a new row at the bottom of the table, move the cursor to the last cell in the table and press Tab.

To insert a new column at the right edge of the table, follow these steps:

1. Click just outside the table's right border.

2. Select Table, Select Column.

3. Select Table, Insert Columns.

MOVING OR COPYING COLUMNS AND ROWS

Here's how to copy or move an entire column or row from one location in a table to another:

1. Select the column or row by dragging over the cells, or by clicking in the column or row and selecting Table, Select Row or Table, Select Column.

2. To copy, press Ctrl+C or click the Copy button on the Standard toolbar. To move, press Ctrl+X or click the Cut button.

3. Move the cursor to the new location for the column or row. (It will be inserted above or to the left of the location of the cursor.)

4. Press Ctrl+V or click the Paste button on the Standard toolbar.

CHANGING COLUMN WIDTH

You can use a dialog box to change column widths. Follow these steps to learn how:

1. Move the cursor to any cell in the column you want to change.

2. Select Table, Cell Height and Width. The Cell Height and Width dialog box appears (see Figure 4.8). If necessary, click the Column tab to display the column options.

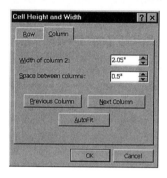

FIGURE 4.8　Changing column width.

3. In the Width Of Column text box, enter the desired column width, or click the up and down arrows to change the setting. Note that the label identifies which column you are working on by number. To automatically adjust the column width to fit the widest cell entry, click the Autofit button.

4. Change the value in the Space Between Columns text box to modify spacing between columns. Changing this setting increases or decreases the amount of space between the text in each cell and the cell's left and right borders.

5. Click Next Column or Previous Column to change the settings for other columns in the table. Click OK. The table changes to reflect the new column settings.

You can quickly change the width of a column with the mouse by pointing at the right border of the column whose width you want to change. The mouse pointer changes to a pair of thin vertical lines with arrowheads pointing left and right. Then, drag the column border to the desired width.

How Wide? When you drag a cell's border to change its width, if no cells are selected, the width changes for the entire table. However, if any cells are selected, the width changes for only the rows in which those cells lie. If you resize a column width and only one row changes, undo your changes (Ctrl+Z), click away from the table to deselect any selected cells, and try again.

APPLYING TABLE BORDERS

Word's default is to place a single, thin border around each cell in a table. However, you can modify the borders or remove them altogether. The techniques for working with table borders are essentially the same as for adding borders to other text. Briefly, here are the steps involved:

1. Select the table cells whose borders you want to modify.

2. Select Format, Borders And Shading to display the Borders and Shading dialog box. Click the Borders tab if necessary.

3. Select the desired border settings, using the Preview box to see how your settings will appear. Click OK.

In a table with no borders, you can display non-printing gridlines on-screen to make it easier to work with the table. Select Table, Show Gridlines to display gridlines. When you finish working with the table, select Table, Hide Gridlines to turn them off.

In this lesson, you learned how to control the Word screen display to suit your working style, how to add tables to your document, and how to edit and format tables.

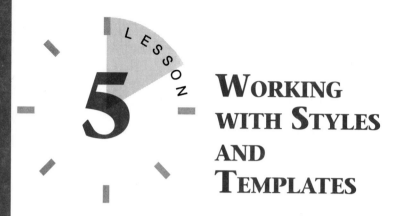

LESSON 5

WORKING WITH STYLES AND TEMPLATES

In this lesson, you learn how to use styles in your documents, how to create new document templates, and how to modify existing templates.

UNDERSTANDING STYLES

Word's styles provide a great deal of power and flexibility when it comes to formatting your document. A style is a collection of formatting specifications that has been assigned a name and saved. For example, a given style could specify 14-point Arial font, 1-inch indent, double line spacing, and full justification. After you define a style, you can quickly apply it to any text in your document. Word has two types of styles:

- Paragraph Styles   Apply to entire paragraphs and can include all aspects of formatting that affect a paragraph's appearance: font, line spacing, indents, tab stops, borders, and so on. Every paragraph has a style; the default paragraph style is called Normal.

- Character Styles   Apply to any section of text and can include any formatting that applies to individual characters: font name and size, underlining, boldface, and so on (in other words, any of the formats that you can assign by selecting Format, Font). There is no default character style.

Applying a style is a lot faster than manually applying individual formatting elements, and it has the added advantage of assuring consistency. If you later modify a style definition, all the text in the document to which that style has been assigned will automatically change to reflect the new style formatting. Word has several predefined styles, and you can create your own.

ASSIGNING A STYLE TO TEXT

To assign a paragraph style to multiple paragraphs, select the paragraphs. To assign a paragraph style to a single paragraph, place the cursor anywhere in the paragraph. To assign a character style, select the text you want the style to affect. Then follow these steps to apply the desired formatting:

1. Click the Style drop-down arrow on the Formatting toolbar to see a list of available styles, with each style name displayed in the style's font. Symbols in the list also indicate whether a style is a paragraph or character style, as well as its font size and justification (see Figure 5.1).

2. Select the desired style by clicking its name. The style is applied to the specified text.

FIGURE 5.1   Select a style from the Style list on the Formatting toolbar.

To remove a character style from text, select the text and apply the character style Default Paragraph Font. This is not really a style; instead it specifies that the formatting defined in the current paragraph style should be used for the text.

Viewing Style Names   The Style list box displays the name of the style assigned to the text where the insertion point is located. If there is text selected or if the insertion point is in text that has a character style applied, the Style list box displays the character style name. Otherwise, it displays the paragraph style of the current paragraph.

CREATING A NEW STYLE

You are not limited to using Word's predefined styles. In fact, creating your own styles is an essential part of getting the most out of Word's style capabilities. One way to create a new style is *by example*, as described in these steps:

1. Place the insertion point in a paragraph to which you want to apply the new style.

2. Format the paragraph as desired. In other words, apply the formatting you want included in the new style definition.

3. With the insertion point anywhere in the paragraph, click the Style list box or press Ctrl+Shift+S (both activate the Style list box).

4. Type a name for the new style and press Enter.

In step 4, make sure you do not enter the name of an existing style. If you do, that style's formatting will be applied to the paragraph, and the formatting changes you made will be lost. If this happens, you can recover the formatting by clicking Edit, Undo. Then repeat steps 3 and 4 and give the style a new and unique name.

Styles For Headings? You may not want to create your own styles for headings; using Word's default style names (Heading 1, Heading 2, and so on) has advantages. If, for example, you use Word's default styles for headings, you can switch to Outline view to see an outline of your document based on the headings. If you make up your own styles for the headings, you can't do that. Another benefit of using Word's predefined heading styles is that by default the heading styles are selected for Word's Index and Table of Contents tools.

You also can create a new style by making formatting entries in dialog boxes. You must use this method to create a character style; it is optional for paragraph styles. You can create a new style from scratch, or you can base it on an existing style. If you choose the latter method, the new style will have all the formatting of the base style plus any additions and changes you make while defining the style. Here are the required steps:

1. Click Format, Style to open the Style dialog box.

2. Click the New button. The New Style dialog box appears (see Figure 5.2).

FIGURE 5.2   The New Style dialog box.

3. Click the Style Type drop-down arrow and select Character or Paragraph from the list to indicate the type of style you're creating.

4. Click the Name text box and type the name for the new style.

5. If you want to base the new style on an existing style, click the Based On drop-down arrow and select the desired base style from the list.

6. If you want the new style to be part of the template that the current document is based on, select the Add To Template check box. If you do not select this check box, the new style will be available only in the current document.

7. (Optional) Select the Automatically Update check box if you want Word to add to the style definition all manual formatting changes you make to paragraphs with this style assigned. (This option is available only for paragraph styles.)

8. Click the Format button and select Font or Border to specify the font and/or border of the new style. As you make formatting changes, the Preview box displays an image of what the style will look like, and the Description area provides a description of the style elements.

9. For paragraph styles only, click the Format button and select Paragraph to set the style's indents and line spacing. Then select Tabs to set the new style's tab stops. Click OK to return to the Style dialog box.

10. Click Apply to assign the new style to the current text or paragraph. Click Close to save the new style definition without assigning it to any text.

MODIFYING A STYLE

You can change the formatting associated with any paragraph or character style, whether it is a style you define or one of Word's predefined styles. When you do so, all text in the document that has the style assigned will be modified. Follow these steps to change a style throughout a document:

1. Click Format, Style to open the Style dialog box (see Figure 5.3).

2. Click the List drop-down arrow and select which styles should be displayed in the Styles list:

   • All Styles   All styles defined in the current document.

   • Styles in Use   Styles assigned to text in the current document.

   • User Defined Styles   All user-defined styles in the current document.

3. In the Styles list, click the name of the style you want to modify.

4. Click the Modify button. The Modify Style dialog box appears; it looks the same as the New Style dialog box (refer to Figure 5.2). Specify the style's new format specifications. Click OK to return to the Style dialog box. Then click Close.

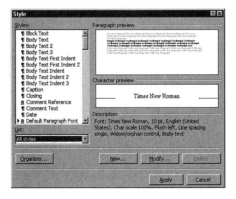

FIGURE 5.3   The Style dialog box.

Fast Style Change A quicker way to change a style is to apply the style to some text in your document and then change that text in your document, and then change that text to the way you want the style to be. Then click in the Style box on the Formatting toolbar so that the style name is highlighted, and press Enter. If you chose the Update Automatically check box in the New Style dialog box (refer to Figure 5.2), the style changes automatically; if you didn't, a dialog box asks whether you want to change the style or revert to the original formatting for that style.

CREATING A NEW TEMPLATE

You learned that every Word document is based on a template, and that Word comes with a variety of predefined templates. You also can create your own templates or modify existing templates to suit your individual needs.

You can create a new template based on an existing template, and the new template will contain all the elements of the base template plus any text or formatting you add. To create a new template from scratch, base it on the Blank Document template. Here are the steps to follow:

1. Select File, New to open the New dialog box (see Figure 5.4).

2. Click the Template option button (in the lower-right corner).

3. If you want the new template based on an existing template, select that template icon in the dialog box. Otherwise, select the Blank Document icon on the General tab. Click OK. A document-editing screen appears with a default name, such as TEMPLATE1.

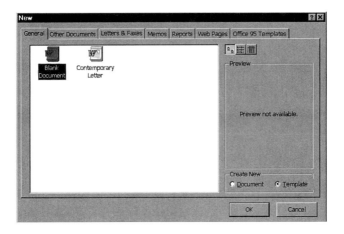

FIGURE 5.4   Creating a new template based on the Blank Document template.

4. Enter the boilerplate text and other items that you want to include in the new template, and then apply formatting to the text as desired. You should also create any styles that you want in the template.

Boilerplate   This is text that you want to appear in every document based on the new template.

5. Select File, Save or click the Save button on the Standard toolbar. The Save As dialog box appears.

6. If necessary, select the folder where you want the new template saved. For example, if it is a template for a letter, you would probably save it in the Letters & Faxes folder.

7. In the File Name text box, enter a descriptive name for the template, using up to 256 characters. Be sure to use a different name from the template you selected in step 3, or the new template will replace the original one.

8. Select Save. Word saves the template under the specified name. It is now available for use each time you start a new document.

In step 6, you must save the template either in the Templates folder or in one of the subfolders beneath it. Each of these subfolders represents a tab in the New dialog box when you start a new template. If you save the template anywhere else, the New dialog box will not show it as a usable template.

MODIFYING AN EXISTING TEMPLATE

Suppose you create your own template, but then you find out that you need to change the boilerplate text slightly. You can retrieve any existing template from disk and modify it. Here's how:

1. Select File, Open to open the Open dialog box.

2. Navigate to the C:\Program Files\Microsoft Office\Templates folder. Open the Files Of Type drop-down list and choose Document Templates.

3. Select the template you want to modify. Click Open. The template opens.

4. Make changes to the template as needed.

5. Select File, Save or click the Save button on the Standard toolbar, and Word saves the modified template to disk.

When you modify a template, changes you make are not reflected in documents that were created based on the template before it was changed. Only new documents will be affected.

CREATING A TEMPLATE FROM A DOCUMENT

Sometimes you will find it useful to create a template based on an existing Word document. Here are the steps to follow:

1. Open the document on which you want to base the new template.

2. Use Word's editing commands to delete any document text and formatting that you do not want to include in the template.

3. Select File, Save As to open the Save As dialog box. Click the Save As Type drop-down arrow and choose Document Template from the list. The Save In box automatically changes to indicate the Templates folder.

4. If appropriate, double-click the name of the folder in which you want to save the template.

5. Type a descriptive name for the template in the File Name text box. Click Save.

In step 3, it's important to select the proper template folder. When you select Document Template, Word automatically switches to the Templates folder. Templates saved in this folder will appear on the General tab in the New dialog box. Because Word organizes templates by category, you may want to place your new template in the appropriate folder because if you don't, you may have trouble finding it later. For example, if you create a template for a memo, save it in the Memos folder so that it will appear on the Memos tab in the New dialog box.

UPDATING A DOCUMENT WHEN THE TEMPLATE CHANGES

If you modify a template, only new documents based on that template will reflect the changes. Existing documents that were based on the old version of the template will not be affected. You can, however, import new styles from a modified template to an existing document. Here's how:

1. Open the document.

2. Select Tools, Templates And Add-ins.

3. Select the Automatically Update Document Styles check box. Click OK.

With this check box selected, the document styles will automatically be updated to reflect the styles in its attached template each time the document is loaded. Other elements of a template, such as boilerplate text, will not be affected.

 Immediate Update   If you want the document to be updated with the latest template styles immediately, you can either close the document and reopen it, or you can attach a different template with the Tools, Templates, and Add-Ins dialog box—and then reattach the original template by marking the Automatically Update Document Styles check box.

In this lesson, you learned how to use styles in your documents, how to create new document templates, and how to modify existing templates.

6

EDITING WORKSHEETS

In this lesson, you learn how to copy, move, and delete data. You also learn how to adjust column width and row height and how to rearrange your worksheet by adding and removing cells, rows, and columns.

COPYING WORKSHEET ENTRIES QUICKLY

You can copy an existing entry into an worksheet's surrounding cells by performing the following steps:

1. Click the fill handle of the cell whose contents you want to copy.

2. Drag the fill handle down or to the right to copy the data to adjacent cells. A bubble appears to let you know exactly what data is being copied to the other cells.

If you're copying a number, a month, or other item that might be interpreted as a series (such as January, February, and so on), but you don't want to create a series—you just want to copy the contents of the cell exactly—press and hold the Ctrl key as you drag the fill handle.

Copying Between Workseets   If you want to copy the contents of cells from one worksheet to one or more worksheets in the workbook, first select the worksheet(s) you want to copy to by clicking the sheet tabs while holding down the Ctrl key. Then select the cells you want to copy. Open the Edit menu, select Fill, and select Across Worksheets. Then select All (to copy both the cells' contents and their formatting), Contents, or Formats, and click OK.

ENTERING A SERIES WITH AUTOFILL

Entering a series (such as January, February, and March or 1994, 1995, 1996, and 1997) is similar to copying a cell's contents. As you drag the fill handle of the original cell, AutoFill does all the work for you, interpreting the first entry and creating a series of entries based on it. For example, if you type Monday in a cell, and then drag the cell's fill handle over some adjacent cells, you'll create the series Monday, Tuesday, Wednesday, etc. As you drag, the bubble let's you know exactly what you're copying so that you can stop at the appropriate cell to create exactly the series you want.

ENTERING A CUSTOM SERIES

Although AutoFill is good for a brief series of entries, you may encounter situations in which you need more control. Excel can handle several different types of series, as shown in Table 6.1.

TABLE 6.1   DATA SERIES

SERIES	INITIAL ENTRIES	RESULTING SERIES
Linear	1, 2	1, 2, 3, 4
	100, 99	100, 99, 98, 97
	1, 3	1, 3, 5, 7
Growth	10, 20	10, 20, 30, 40
	10, 50	10, 50, 90, 130
Date	Mon, Wed	Mon, Wed, Fri
	Feb, May	Feb, May, Aug
	Qtr1, Qtr3	Qtr1, Qtr3, Qtr1
	1992, 1995	1992, 1995, 1998

Basically, you make two sample entries for your series in adjacent cells, and Excel uses them to calculate the rest of the series. Here's what you do:

1. Enter the first value in one cell.

2. Move to the second cell and enter the next value in the series.

3. Select both cells by dragging over them. Excel highlights the cells.

4. Drag the fill handle over as many adjacent cells as necessary. Excel computes your series and fills the selected cells with the appropriate values, as shown in Figure 6.1.

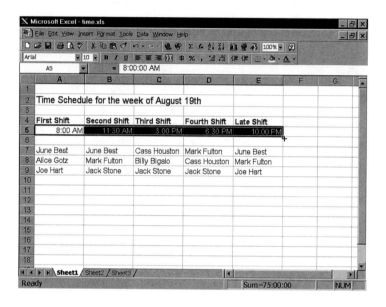

FIGURE 6.1   Drag to create your series.

ENTERING THE SAME DATA OVER AND OVER WITH AUTOCOMPLETE

When you type the first few letters of an entry, AutoComplete intelligently completes the entry for you based on the entries you've already made in that particular column. AutoComplete works with data entered in columns only, not rows. For example, suppose you want to enter the countries of origin for a series of packages. You type the name of a country once, and the next time you start to type that entry, AutoComplete inserts it for you.

By default, AutoComplete is always turned on, so you don't have to worry about that. However, if it drives you crazy, you can turn it off with the Tools, Options command. Click the Edit tab and click the Enable AutoComplete For Cell Values option to turn it off.

Follow these steps to try out AutoFormat:

1. Type England into a cell and press the down-arrow key to move to the next cell down. Type Spain and press the down-arrow key again. Then type Italy and press the down-arrow key.

2. Type e again, and "England" appears in the cell. Press Enter to accept the entry. (Likewise, the next time you type i or s, "Italy" or "Spain" will appear.)

3. To see a list of AutoComplete entries, right-click the next cell and select Pick From List from the shortcut menu. Excel shows you a PickList of entries (in alphabetical order) that it has automatically created from the words you've typed in the column.

4. Click a word in the PickList to insert it in the selected cell.

EDITING DATA ENTRIES

After you have entered data into a cell, you may edit it in either the Formula bar or in the cell itself.

To edit an entry in Excel:

1. Click the cell in which you want to edit data.

2. To begin editing, click the Formula bar, press F2, or double-click the cell. This puts you in Edit mode; the word Edit appears in the Status bar.

3. Press $\Leftarrow$ or $\Rightarrow$ to move the insertion point within the entry. Press the Backspace key to delete characters to the left of the insertion point; press the Delete key to delete characters to the right. Then type any characters you want to add.

4. Click the Enter button on the Formula bar or press Enter on the keyboard to accept your changes.

   Or, if you change your mind and you no longer want to edit your entry, click the Cancel button or press Esc.

SELECTING CELLS

To copy, move, or delete the data in several cells at one time, you must select those cells first. Then you can perform the appropriate action. Here are the various selection options:

- To select a single cell, click it.

- To select adjacent cells (a range), click the upper-left cell in the group and drag down to the lower-right cell to select additional cells.

- To select nonadjacent cells, press and hold the Ctrl key as you click individual cells.

- To select an entire row or column of cells, click the row or column header. To select adjacent rows or columns, drag over their headers. To select non-adjacent rows or columns, press Ctrl and click each header that you want to select.

DELETING DATA

To delete the data in a cell or cells, you can just select them and press Delete. However, Excel offers additional options for deleting cells:

- With the Edit, Clear command, you can choose to delete just the formatting of a cell (or an attached comment), instead of deleting its contents. The formatting of a cell includes the cell's color, border style, numeric format, font size, and so on.

- With the Edit, Delete command, you remove cells and everything in them.

To use the Clear command to remove the formatting of a cell or a note, follow these steps:

1. Select the cells you want to clear.

2. Open the Edit menu and select Clear. The Clear submenu appears.

3. Select the desired clear option: All (which clears the cells of its contents, formatting, and notes), Formats, Contents, or Comments.

ADJUSTING COLUMN WIDTH AND ROW HEIGHT

You can adjust the width of a column or the height of a row by using a dialog box or by dragging with the mouse.

Why Bother? You might not want to bother adjusting the row height because it's automatically adjusted as you change font size. However, if a column's width is not as large as its data, that data may not be displayed and may appear as ########. In such a case, you must adjust the width of the column in order for the data to be displayed at all.

Here's how you adjust the row height or column width with the mouse:

1. To change the row height or column width for a single row or column, skip to step 2. To change the height or width of two or more rows for columns, select them first by dragging over the row or column headings.

2. Position the mouse pointer over one of the row heading or column heading borders as shown in Figure 6.2. (Use the right border of the column heading to adjust column width; use the bottom border of the row heading to adjust the row height.)

3. Drag the border to the size you need it.

4. Release the mouse button, and Excel adjusts the row height or column width.

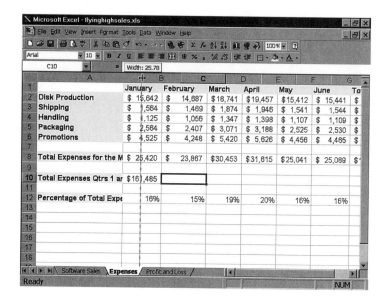

FIGURE 6.2 The mouse pointer changes to a double-headed arrow when you move it over a border in the row or column heading.

AutoFit Cells To quickly make a column as wide as its widest entry using Excel's AutoFit feature, double-click the right border of the column heading. To make a row as tall as its tallest entry, double-click the bottom border of the row heading. To change more than one column or row at a time, drag over the desired row or column headings, and then double-click the bottommost or rightmost heading border.

INSERTING CELLS

Sometimes, you will need to insert information into a worksheet, right in the middle of existing data. With the Insert command, you can insert one or more cells, or entire rows or columns.

Shifting Cells   Inserting cells in the middle of existing data will cause the data in existing cells to shift down a row or over a column. If your worksheet contains formulas that rely on the contents of the shifting cells, this could throw off the calculations. Be sure to check all formulas that might be affected.

To insert a single cell or a group of cells, follow these steps:

1. Select the cell(s) where you want the new cell(s) inserted. Excel will insert the same number of cells as you select.

2. Open the Insert menu and choose Cells. The Insert dialog box shown in Figure 6.3 appears.

3. Select Shift Cells Right or Shift Cells Down. Click OK. Excel inserts the cell(s) and shifts the data in the other cells in the specified direction.

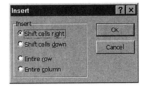

FIGURE 6.3   The Insert dialog box.

MERGING CELLS

In Excel 97, you can merge the data worksheets in one cell with other cells to form a big cell that is easier to use. Merging cells is especially handy when creating a decorative title for the top of your worksheet (see Figure 6.4 for an example). Within a single merged cell, you can quickly change the font, point size, color, and border style of your title.

To create a title with merged cells, follow these steps:

1. Type your title in the upper-left cell of the range you want to use for your heading. If you have a multiline title, like the one in Figure 6.4, press Alt+Enter to insert each new line.

2. Select the range in which you want to place your title.

3. Open the Format menu and select Cells. The Format Cells dialog box appears.

4. Click the Alignment tab.

5. Click Merge Cells. You may also want to make adjustments to the text within the merged cells. For example, you may want to select Center in the Vertical drop-down list to center the text vertically within the cell.

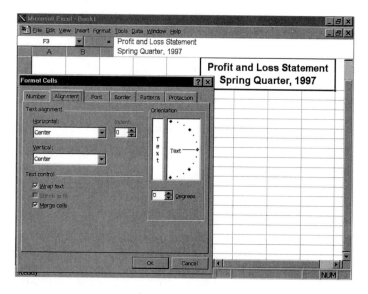

FIGURE 6.4 Merge cells to form a single cell.

6. Click OK when you're done. The selected cells are merged into a single cell, which you can format as needed.

You can merge selected cells and center the data in the left-most cell by clicking the Merge and Center button on the Formatting toolbar.

Removing Cells

Sometimes you will want to eliminate cells completely. When you do, Excel removes the cells and adjusts the data in surrounding cells to fill the gap.

If you want to remove the cells completely, perform the following steps:

1. Select the range of cells you want to remove.

2. Open the Edit menu and choose Delete. The Delete dialog box appears.

3. Select the desired Delete option: Shift Cells Left or Shift Cells Up. Click OK.

Inserting Rows and Columns

Inserting entire rows and columns in your worksheet is easy. Here's what you do:

1. To insert a single row or column, select the cell to the left of which you want to insert a column, or above where you want to insert a row.

   To insert multiple columns or rows, select the number of columns or rows you want to insert. To insert columns, drag over the column letters at the top of the worksheet. To insert rows, drag over the row numbers. For example, select three column letters or row numbers to insert three rows or columns.

2. Open the Insert menu. Select Rows or Columns. Excel inserts the row(s) or column(s) and shifts the adjacent rows down or the adjacent columns right. The inserted rows or columns contain the same formatting as the cells

you selected in step 1. Figure 6.5 simulates a worksheet before and after two rows were inserted.

	A	B	C	D	E	F	G	H
1		January	February	March	April	May	June	
2	Disk Production	$15,642	$14,687	$18,741	$19,457	$15,412	$ 15,441	
3	Packaging	$ 2,564	$ 2,407	$ 3,071	$ 3,188	$ 2,525	$ 2,530	
4	Promotions	$ 4,525	$ 4,248	$ 5,420	$ 5,626	$ 4,456	$ 4,465	
5								
6	Total Expenses	$22,731	$21,342	$27,232	$28,271	$22,393	$ 22,436	
7								
8	Disk Production	$15,642	$14,687	$18,741	$19,457	$15,412	$ 15,441	
9								
10								
11	Packaging	$ 2,564	$ 2,407	$ 3,071	$ 3,188	$ 2,525	$ 2,530	
12	Promotions	$ 4,525	$ 4,525	$ 4,525	$ 4,525	$ 4,525	$ 4,525	
13								
14	Total Expenses	$22,731	$21,619	$26,337	$27,170	$22,462	$ 22,496	
15								
16								
17								
18								

FIGURE 6.5   Inserting two rows in a worksheet.

Shortcut Insert   To quickly insert rows or columns, select one or more rows or columns. Then right-click one of them and choose Insert from the shortcut menu.

REMOVING ROWS AND COLUMNS

Deleting rows and columns is similar to deleting cells. When you delete a row, the rows below the deleted row move up to fill the space. When you delete a column, the columns to the right shift left.

Follow these steps to delete a row or column:

1. Click the row number or column letter of the row or column you want to delete. You can select more than one row or column by dragging over the row numbers or column letters.

2. Open the Edit menu and choose Delete. Excel deletes the row(s) or column(s) and renumbers the remaining rows and columns sequentially. All cell references in formulas and names in formulas are updated appropriately, unless they are absolute ($) values.

In this lesson, you learn how to copy, move, and delete data. You also learn how to adjust column width and row height and how to rearrange your worksheet by adding and removing cells, rows, and columns.

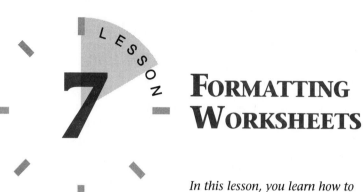

FORMATTING WORKSHEETS

In this lesson, you learn how to customize the appearance of numbers and text in your worksheet and how to add pizzazz to your worksheets.

FORMATTING VALUES

Numeric values are usually more than just numbers. They represent a dollar value, a date, a percent, or some other value. Excel offers a wide range of number formats, which are listed in Table 7.1.

TABLE 7.1 EXCEL'S NUMBER FORMATS

NUMBER FORMAT	EXAMPLES	DESCRIPTION
General	7.6 $456,908.00	Excel displays your value as you enter it. In other words, this format displays currency or percent signs only if you enter them yourself.
Number	3400.50 (-120.39)	The default Number format has two decimal places. Negative numbers appear in red and in parentheses, preceded by a minus sign.
Currency	$3,400.50 ($3,400.50)	The default Currency format has two decimal places and a dollar sign. Negative numbers appear in red and in parentheses.

NUMBER FORMAT	EXAMPLES	DESCRIPTION
Accounting	$ 3,400.00 $ 978.21	Use this format to align dollar signs and decimal points in a column. The default Accounting format has two decimal places and a dollar sign.
Date	11/7	The default Date format is the month and day separated by a slash; however, you can select from numerous other formats.
Time	10:00	The default Time format is the hour and minutes separated by a colon; however, you can opt to display seconds, AM, or PM.
Percentage	99.50%	The default Percentage format has two decimal places. Excel multiplies the value in a cell by 100 and displays the result with a percent sign.
Fraction	1/2	The default Fraction format is up to one digit on either side of the slash. Use this format to display the number of digits you want on either side of the slash and the fraction type (such as halves, quarters, eighths, and so on).
Scientific	3.40E+03	The default Scientific format has two decimal places. Use this format to display numbers in scientific notation.
Text	135RV90	Use Text format to display both text and numbers in a cell as text. Excel displays the entry exactly as you type it.

continued

TABLE 7.1 CONTINUED

NUMBER FORMAT	EXAMPLES	DESCRIPTION
Special	02110	This format is specifically designed to display zip codes, phone numbers, and Social Security numbers correctly, so that you don't have to enter any special characters, such as hyphens.
Custom	00.0%	Use Custom format to create your own number format. You can use any of the format codes in the Type list and then make changes to those codes. The # symbol represents a number placeholder, and 0 represents a zero placeholder.

After deciding on a suitable numeric format, follow these steps:

1. Select the cell or range that contains the values you want to format.

2. Open the Format menu and select Cells. The Format Cells dialog box appears, as shown in Figure 7.1. Click the Number tab.

3. In the Category list, select the numeric format category you want to use. The sample box displays the default format for that category.

4. Make changes to the format as needed. Click OK or press Enter. Excel reformats the selected cells based on your selections.

 Removing Formatting   If you want to remove a number format from a cell (and return it to General format), select the cells whose formatting you want to remove, open the Edit menu, select Clear, then select Formats.

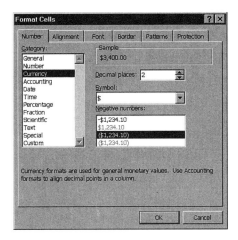

FIGURE 7.1   The Format Cells dialog box with the Number tab displayed.

MAKING TEXT LOOK DIFFERENT

When you type text or numbers, Excel automatically formats it in the defaults, which don't look very fancy.

You can change the following text attributes to improve the appearance of your text or set it apart from other text:

- Font   A typeface—for example, Arial, Courier, or Times New Roman.

- Font Style   For example, Bold, Italic, Underline, or Strikethrough.

Text Underline versus Cell Border   You can add underlining to important information in one of two ways. With the underline format, a line (or lines, depending on which underline format you choose) is placed under the cell's contents. This is different from adding a line to the bottom of a cell's border.

- Size   For example, 10-point, 12-point, or 20-point. (The higher the point size, the bigger the text is. There are approximately 72 points in an inch.)

- Color   For example, Red, Magenta, or Cyan.

- Alignment   For example, centered, left aligned, or right aligned within the cell.

The quickest way to format cells is to use the Formatting toolbar shown in Figure 7.2.

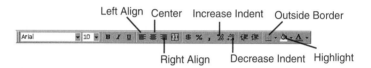

Figure 7.2   Use the Formatting toolbar to quickly make font changes.

Figure 7.3 shows a worksheet after some attributes have been changed for selected text.

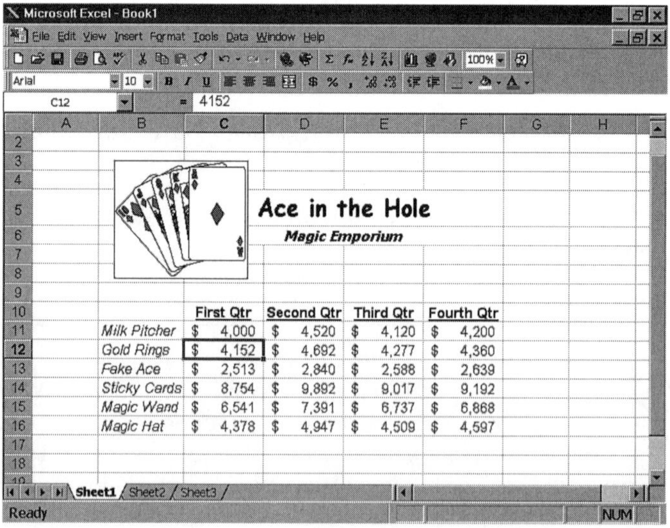

Figure 7.3   A sampling of several text attributes.

ALIGNING TEXT IN CELLS

When you enter data into an Excel worksheet, that data is aligned automatically. Text is aligned on the left, and numbers are aligned on the right. Both text and numbers are initially set at the bottom of the cells. However, you can change both the vertical and the horizontal alignment of data in your cells.

Follow these steps to change the alignment:

1. Select the cell or range you want to align. If you want to center a title or other text over a range of cells, select the entire range of blank cells in which you want the text centered, including the cell that contains the text you want to center.

2. Pull down the Format menu and select Cells, or press Ctrl+1. The Format Cells dialog box appears.

3. Click the Alignment tab. The alignment options appear in front (see Figure 7.4).

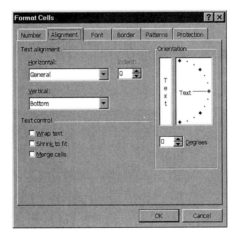

Figure 7.4   The Alignment options.

4. Choose from the following options and option groups to set the alignment:

Horizontal lets you specify a left/right alignment in the cell(s). (The Center Across selection centers a title or other text within a range of cells.)

Vertical lets you specify how you want the text aligned in relation to the top and bottom of the cell(s).

Orientation lets you flip the text sideways or print it from top to bottom (instead of left to right). This option is new to Excel 97.

Wrap Text tells Excel to wrap long lines of text within a cell without changing the width of the cell. (Normally, Excel displays all text in a cell on one line.)

Shrink to Fit shrinks the text to fit within the cell's current width. If the cell's width is adjusted, the text increases or decreases in size accordingly.

Merge Cells combines several cells into a single cell. All data is overlaid, except for the cell in the upper-left corner of the selected cells.

5. Click OK or press Enter.

New to Excel 97 is the capability to indent your text within a cell. If you're typing a paragraph worth of information into a single cell, you can indent that paragraph by selecting left alignment from the Horizontal list box in the Format Cells dialog box (as explained in the previous section). After selecting left alignment, set the amount of indent you want with the Indent spin box.

In addition, you can add an indent quickly by clicking the following buttons on the Formatting toolbar:

- Decrease Indent   Removes an indent or creates a negative indent.

- Increase Indent   Adds an indent.

ADDING BORDERS TO CELLS

As you work with your worksheet on-screen, you'll notice that each cell is identified by gridlines that surround the cell. Normally, these gridlines do not print; and even if you choose to print them, they may appear washed out. To have more well-defined lines appear on the printout (or on-screen, for that matter), you can add borders to selected cells or entire cell ranges. A border can appear on all four sides of a cell or only on selected sides, whichever you prefer.

 The Gridlines Don't Print?   In Excel 97, as in Excel 95, the gridlines do not print by default. But if you want to try printing your worksheet with gridlines first just to see what it looks like, open the File menu, select Page Setup, click the Sheet tab, select Gridlines, and click OK.

To add borders to a cell or range, perform the following steps:

1. Select the cell(s) around which you want a border to appear.

2. Open the Format menu and choose Cells. The Format Cells dialog box appears.

3. Click the Border tab to see the Border options shown in Figure 7.5.

4. Select the desired position, style (thickness), and color for the border. You can click inside the Border box itself, or you can click a preset border pattern button to add your border. Click OK or press Enter.

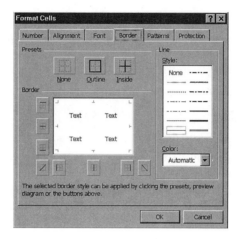

FIGURE 7.5 Choose border options from the Format Cells dialog box.

 Hiding Gridlines When adding borders to a worksheet, you might need to hide the gridlines to get a better idea of how the borders will look when printed. Open the Tools menu, select Options, click the View tab, and select Gridlines to remove the check mark from the check box. Of course, selecting this option has no effect on whether or not the gridlines actually print, only on whether or not they are displayed on-screen.

To add borders quickly, select the cells around which you want the border to appear, and then click the Borders drop-down arrow in the Formatting toolbar. Click the desired border. If you click the Borders button itself (instead of the arrow), Excel automatically adds the border line you last chose to the selected cells.

ADDING SHADING TO CELLS

For a simple but dramatic effect, you can add shading to your worksheets. With shading, you can add a color or gray shading to a cell. You can add colors at full strength or partial strength to create the exact effect you want. To lessen the strength of the cell color you select, you add your shading with a pattern, such as a diagonal. Figure 7.6 illustrates some of the effects you can create with shading.

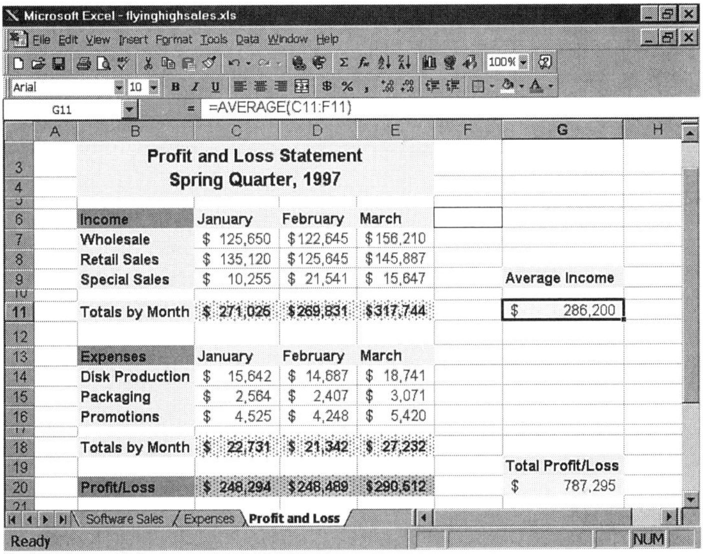

FIGURE 7.6 A worksheet with added shading.

Follow these steps to add shading to a cell or range. As you make your selections, keep in mind that if you plan to print your worksheet with a black-and-white printer, your pretty colors may not be different enough to create the effect you want. Select colors that contrast well in value (intensity), and use the Print Preview command to view your results in black-and- white before you print.

1. Select the cell(s) you want to shade.

2. Open the Format menu and choose Cells.

3. Click the Patterns tab. Excel displays the shading options (see Figure 7.7).

4. Click the Pattern drop-down arrow, and you will see a grid that contains all the colors from the color palette, as well as patterns. Select the shading color and pattern you want to use. The Color options let you choose a color for the overall shading. The Pattern options let you select a black-and-white or colored pattern that lies on top of the overall shading. A preview of the result appears in the Sample box. When you like the results you see, click OK or press Enter.

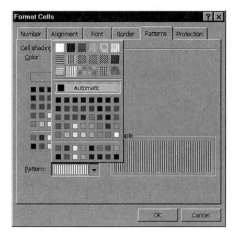

Figure 7.7   Selecting a shading and a pattern.

A quick way to add cell shading (without a pattern) is to select the cells you want to shade, click the Fill Color drop-down arrow, and click the color you want to use.

Using AutoFormat

Excel offers the AutoFormat feature, which takes some of the pain out of formatting. AutoFormat provides you with 16 predesigned table formats that you can apply to a worksheet.

To use predesigned formats, perform the following steps:

1. Select the worksheet(s) and cell(s) that contain the data you want to format.

2. Open the Format menu and choose AutoFormat. The AutoFormat dialog box appears, as shown in Figure 7.8.

3. In the Table Format list, choose the predesigned format you want to use. When you select a format, Excel shows you what it will look like in the Sample area.

4. To exclude certain elements from AutoFormat, click the Options button and choose the formats you want to turn off.

5. Click OK, and Excel formats your table to make it look like the one in the preview area.

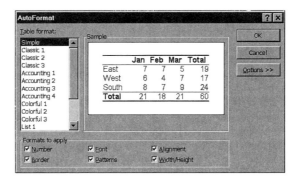

FIGURE 7.8   Use the AutoFormat dialog box to select a prefab format.

Deformatting an AutoFormat   If you don't like what AutoFormat did to your worksheet, select the table, open the Format menu, and choose AutoFormat. From the Table Format list, choose None to remove the AutoFormat.

COPYING FORMATS WITH FORMAT PAINTER

Excel gives you two ways to copy and paste formatting:

- You can use the Edit, Copy command and then the Edit Paste Special command and select Formats from the Paste options in the Paste Special dialog box.

- You can use the Format Painter button in the Standard toolbar.

The Format Painter lets you quickly copy and paste formats that you have already used in a workbook. Because the Format Painter button is faster, I'll give you the steps you need to paint formats.

1. Select the cell(s) that contain the formatting you want to copy and paste.

2. Click the Format Painter button on the Standard toolbar. Excel copies the formatting. The mouse pointer changes into a paintbrush with a plus sign next to it.

3. Click and drag over the cells to which you want to apply the copied formatting.

4. Release the mouse button, and Excel copies the formatting and applies it to the selected cells.

APPLYING CONDITIONAL FORMATTING

If you want to highlight particular values in your worksheet, you can use conditional formatting. For example, if you want to highlight all sales figures under a particular mark, you could apply a conditional red shading.

To apply conditional formatting, follow these steps:

1. Select the cells you want to format.

2. Open the Format menu and select Conditional Formatting. The Conditional Formatting dialog box appears, as shown in Figure 7.9.

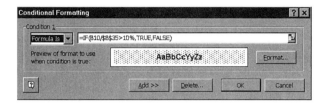

Figure 7.9 Apply formats conditionally to highlight certain values.

3. To apply a format based on the value found in a selected cell, choose Cell Value Is from the Condition 1 list.

   To apply a format based on the value found in a cell outside the selected range, select Formula Is from the Condition 1 list.

4. Enter the value or formula you want to use as the condition that determines when Excel can apply the formatting you select. If you choose to use a formula, be sure to include the beginning equal (=) sign.

5. Click the Format button and select the format you want to apply when the condition is true. Click OK to return to the Conditional Formatting dialog box.

6. (Optional) If you want to add more than one condition, click Add. Then repeat steps 3 and 4 to add the condition.

7. When you finish adding conditions, click OK.

You can copy the conditional formatting from one cell to other cells using the Format Painter button. Simply click the cell whose formatting you want to copy and click the Format Painter button. Then drag over the cells to which you want to copy the formatting.

In this lesson, you learned how to customize the appearance of numbers and text in your worksheet and how to add pizzazz to your worksheets.

USING
FORMULAS AND
FUNCTIONS

In this lesson, you learn how to use formulas in your worksheets how to perform calculations with functions.

UNDERSTANDING FORMULAS

Worksheets use formulas to perform calculations on the data you enter. With formulas, you can perform addition, subtraction, multiplication, and division by using the values contained in various cells.

Formulas typically consist of one or more cell addresses or values and a mathematical operator, such as + (addition), - (subtraction), * (multiplication), or / (division). For example, if you want to determine the average of the three values contained in cells A1, B1, and C1, type the following formula in the cell where you want the result to appear:

=(A1+B1+C1)/3

Figure 8.1 shows several formulas in action. Study the formulas and their results. Table 8.1 lists the mathematical operators you can use to create formulas.

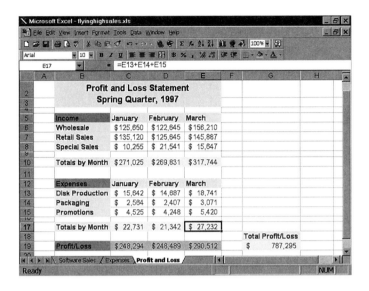

FIGURE 8.1   Type a formula in the cell where you want the resulting value to appear.

TABLE 8.1   EXCEL'S MATHEMATICAL OPERATORS

OPERATOR	PERFORMS	SAMPLE FORMULA	RESULT
^	Exponentiation	=A1^3	Enters the result of raising the value in cell A1 to the third power.
+	Addition	=A1+A2	Enters the total of the values in cells A1 and A2.
-	Subtraction	=A1-A2	Subtracts the value in cell A2 from the value in cell A1.
*	Multiplication	=A2*3	Multiplies the value in cell A2 by 3.

continued

TABLE 8.1 CONTINUED

OPERATOR	PERFORMS	SAMPLE FORMULA	RESULT
/	Division	=A1/50	Divides the value in cell A1 by 50.
	Combination	=(A1+A2 +A3)/3	Determines the average of the values in cells A1 through A3.

ORDER OF OPERATIONS

Excel performs the operations within a formula in the following order: equations within parentheses, exponentiation, multiplication and division, and then addition and subtraction.

For example, given the formula =C2+B8*4+D10, Excel computes the value of B8*4, then adds that to C2, and then adds D10. Keep this order of operations in mind when you are creating equations because it determines the result.

If you don't take this order into consideration, you could run into problems when entering your formulas. For example, if you want to determine the average of the values in cells A1, B1, and C1, and you enter =A1+B1+C1/3, you'll get the wrong answer. The value in C1 will be divided by 3, and that result will be added to A1+B1. To determine the total of A1 through C1 first, you must enclose that group of values in parentheses, as in =(A1+B1+C1)/3.

ENTERING FORMULAS

You can enter formulas in either of two ways: by typing the formula or by selecting cell references. To type a formula, perform the following steps:

1. Select the cell in which you want the formula's calculation to appear.

2. Type the equal sign (=). Type the formula. The formula appears in the Formula bar.

3. Press Enter or click the Enter button (the check mark), and Excel calculates the result.

 Unwanted Formula   If you start to enter a formula and then decide you don't want to use it, you can skip entering the formula by pressing Esc or by clicking the Cancel button.

To enter a formula by selecting cell references, take the following steps:

1. Select the cell in which you want the formula's result to appear.

2. Type the equal sign (=).

3. Click the cell with the address you want to appear first in the formula. The cell address appears in the Formula bar.

 Name That Cell   If you plan to use a particular cell in several formulas, you can give it a name, such as "Income." Then you can use the name in the formula, as in =Income+$12.50. To name a cell, use the Insert, Name, Define command.

4. Type a mathematical operator after the value to indicate the next operation you want to perform. The operator appears in the Formula bar.

5. Continue clicking cells and typing operators until the formula is complete.

6. Press Enter to accept the formula or Esc to cancel the operation.

You can view the sum of a range of cells simply by selecting the cells and looking at the status bar, as shown in Figure 8.2. You can also view the average, minimum, maximum, and the count of a range of cells. To do so, right-click the status bar and select the option you want from the shortcut menu that appears.

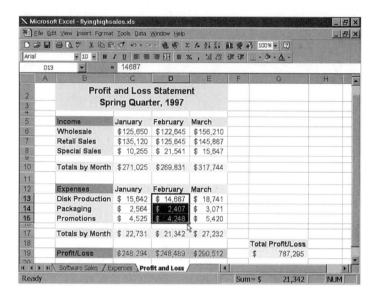

FIGURE 8.2   View a sum without entering a formula.

 Error!   If ERR appears in a cell, make sure that you did not commit one of these common errors: try to divide by zero, use a blank cell as a divisor, refer to a blank cell, delete a cell used in a formula, or include a reference to the cell in which the answer appears.

DISPLAYING FORMULAS

Normally, Excel does not display the actual formula in a cell. Instead, it displays the result of the calculation. You can view the formula by selecting the cell and looking in the Formula bar. However, if you're trying to review the formulas in a large worksheet, it might be easier if you could see them all at once (or print them). If you want to view formulas in a worksheet, follow these steps:

1. Open the Tools menu and choose Options. Click the View tab.

2. In the Window Options area, click to select the Formulas check box. Click OK.

EDITING FORMULAS

Editing a formula is the same as editing any entry in Excel. The following steps show you how to do it:

1. Select the cell that contains the formula you want to edit.

2. Click in the Formula bar or press F2 to enter Edit mode.

 Quick In-Cell Editing To quickly edit the contents of a cell, double-click the cell or press F2. The insertion point appears inside the cell, and you can make any necessary changes.

3. Press the left arrow key [lf] or right arrow key [rt] to move the insertion point. Then use the Backspace key to delete characters to the left, or use the Delete key to delete characters to the right. Type any additional characters.

4. When you finish editing the data, click the Enter button on the Formula bar or press Enter to accept your changes.

COPYING FORMULAS

When you copy a formula, the formula is adjusted to fit the location of the cell to which it is copied. For example, if you copy the formula =C2+C3 from cell C4 to cell D4, the formula is adjusted for column D: it becomes =D2+D3. This enables you to copy similar formulas (such as the totals for a range of sales items) into a range of cells.

You can copy formulas by using the Copy and Paste buttons, but the following presents an even faster way.

1. Click the cell that contains the formula you want to copy.

2. Hold down the Ctrl key and drag the cell's border to the cell to which you want to copy your formula.

3. Release the mouse button, and Excel copies the formula to the new location.

If you want to copy a formula to a neighboring range of cells, follow these steps:

1. Click the cell that contains the formula you want to copy.

2. Move the mouse pointer over the fill handle.

3. Drag the fill handle across the cells into which you want to copy the formula.

 Get an Error?   If you get an error after copying a formula, verify the cell references in the copied formula. See the next section for more details.

USING RELATIVE AND ABSOLUTE CELL ADDRESSES

When you copy a formula from one place in the worksheet to another, Excel adjusts the cell references in the formulas relative to their new positions in the worksheet. For example, in Figure 8.3, cell B8 contains the formula =B2+B3+B4+B5+B6, which computes the total expenses for January. If you copy that formula to cell C8 (to determine the total expenses for February), Excel automatically changes the formula to =C2+C3+C4+C5+C6. This is how relative cell addresses work.

	X Microsoft Excel - flyinghighsales.xls						

Arial   10   B I U

TotalExpensesFeb   =C2+C3+C4+C5+C6

	A	B	C	D	E	F	G
1		January	February	March	April	May	June
2	Disk Production	$ 15,642	$ 14,687	$18,741	$19,457	$15,412	$ 15,44
3	Shipping	$ 1,564	$ 1,469	$ 1,874	$ 1,946	$ 1,541	$ 1,54
4	Handling	$ 1,125	$ 1,056	$ 1,347	$ 1,398	$ 1,107	$ 1,10
5	Packaging	$ 2,564	$ 2,407	$ 3,071	$ 3,188	$ 2,525	$ 2,53
6	Promotions	$ 4,525	$ 4,248	$ 5,420	$ 5,626	$ 4,456	$ 4,46
7							
8	Total Expenses for the Month	$ 25,420	$ 23,867	$30,453	$31,615	$25,041	$ 25,08
9							
10	Total Expenses Qtrs 1 and 2	$ 161,485					
11							
12	Percentage of Total Expenses	16%	15%	19%	20%	16%	16
13							
14							
15							
16							
17							
18							

Software Sales **Expenses** Profit and Loss

Ready   NUM

FIGURE 8.3 Excel adjusts cell references when you copy formulas to different cells.

Sometimes you may not want the cell references to be adjusted when you copy formulas. That's when absolute cell references become important.

Absolute Versus Relative An absolute reference is a cell reference in a formula that does not change when copied to a new location. A relative reference is a cell reference in a formula that is adjusted when the formula is copied.

In the example shown in Figure 8.3, the formulas in cells B12, C12, D12, E12, F12, and G12 contain an absolute reference to cell B10, which holds the total expenses for quarters 1 and 2. (The formulas in B12, C12, D12, E12, F12, and G12 divide the sums from row 8 of each column by the contents of cell B10.) If you didn't use an absolute reference when you copied the formula from B10 to C10, the cell reference would be incorrect, and you would get an error message.

To make a cell reference in a formula absolute, you add a $ (dollar sign) before the letter and number that make up the cell address. For example, the formula in B12 would read as follows:

=B8/B10

You can type the dollar signs yourself, or you can press F4 after typing the cell address.

Some formulas use mixed references. For example, the column letter might be an absolute reference, and the row number might be a relative reference, as in the formula $A2/2. If you entered this formula in cell C2 and then copied it to cell D10, the result would be the formula $A10/2. The row reference (row number) would be adjusted, but the column reference (the letter A) would not be.

CHANGING THE CALCULATION SETTING

Excel recalculates the formulas in a worksheet every time you edit a value in a cell. However, on a large worksheet, you may not want Excel to recalculate until you have entered all of your changes. For example, if you are entering a lot of changes to a worksheet that contains many formulas, you can speed up the response time by changing from automatic to manual recalculation. To change the recalculation setting, take the following steps:

1. Open the Tools menu and choose Options.

2. Click the Calculation tab to see the options shown in Figure 8.4.

3. Select one of the following Calculation options:

    Automatic   This is the default setting. It recalculates the entire workbook each time you edit or enter a formula.

    Automatic Except Tables   This automatically recalculates everything except formulas in a data table.

    Manual   This option tells Excel to recalculate only when you say so. To recalculate, press F9 or choose the Tools, Options, Calculation command and click the Calc Now button.

When this option is selected, you can turn the Recalculate Before Save option off or on.

4. Click OK.

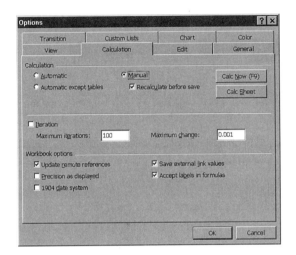

FIGURE 8.4 Change your calculation setting in the Options dialog box.

UNDERSTANDING FUNCTIONS

Functions are complex ready-made formulas that perform a series of operations on a specified range of values. For example, to determine the sum of a series of numbers in cells A1 through H1, you can enter the function =SUM(A1:H1) instead of entering =A1+B1+C1 and so on. Functions can use range references (such as B1:B3), range names (such as SALES), or numerical values (such as 585.86).

Every function consists of the following three elements:

- The = sign indicates that what follows is a function (formula).

- The function name, such as SUM, indicates which operation will be performed.

- The argument, such as (A1:H1), indicates the cell addresses of the values on which the function will act. The argument is often a range of cells, but it can be much more complex.

You can enter functions either by typing them in cells or by using the Function Wizard, as you'll see later in this lesson.

Table 8.2 shows Excel's most common functions that you'll use in your worksheets.

TABLE 8.2   EXCEL'S MOST COMMON FUNCTIONS

FUNCTION	EXAMPLE	DESCRIPTION
AVERAGE	=AVERAGE(B4:B9)	Calculates the mean or average of a group of numbers.
COUNT	=COUNT(A3:A7)	Counts the numeric values in a range. For example, if a range contains some cells with text and other cells with numbers, you can count how many numbers are in that range.
COUNTA	=COUNTA(B4:B10)	Counts all cells in a range that are not blank. For example, if a range contains some cells with text and other cells with numbers, you can count how many cells in that range contain text.
IF	=IF(A3>=100,A3 *2,A2*2)	Allows you to place a condition on a formula. In this example, if A3 is greater than or equal to 100, the formula A3*2 is used. If A3 is less than 100, the formula A2*2 is used instead.

FUNCTION	EXAMPLE	DESCRIPTION
MAX	=MAX(B4:B10)	Returns the maximum value in a range of cells.
MIN	=MIN(B4:B10)	Returns the minimum value in a range of cells.
PMT	=PMT(rate,nper,pv)	Calculates the periodic payment on a loan when you enter the interest rate, number of periods, and principal as arguments. Example: =PMT(.0825/12,360,180000) for 30-year loan at 8.25% for $180,000.
PMT	=PMT(rate,nper,,fv)	Calculates the deposit needed each period to reach some future value. Example: =PMT(.07/12,60,,10000) calculates the deposit needed to accumulate $10,000 at an annual rate of 7%, making monthly payments for 5 years (60 months).
SUM	=SUM(A1:A10)	Calculates the total in a range of cells.
SUMIF	=SUMIF(rg,criteria,sumrg)	Calculates the total of the range rg for each corresponding cell in sumrg that matches the specified criteria. For example, =SUMIF(A2:A4,>100,B2:B4) adds the cells in the range A2:A4 whose corresponding cell in column B is greater than 100.

USING AUTOSUM

Because SUM is one of the most commonly used functions, Excel provides a fast way to enter it—you simply click the AutoSum button in the Standard toolbar. Based on the currently selected cell, AutoSum guesses which cells you want summed. If AutoSum selects an incorrect range of cells, you can edit the selection.

To use AutoSum, follow these steps:

1. Select the cell in which you want the sum inserted. Try to choose a cell at the end of a row or column of data; doing so will help AutoSum guess which cells you want added together.

2. Click the AutoSum button in the Standard toolbar. AutoSum inserts =SUM and the range address of the cells to the left of or above the selected cell (see Figure 8.5).

3. If the range Excel selected is incorrect, drag over the range you want to use, or click in the Formula bar and edit the formula.

4. Click the Enter button in the Formula bar or press Enter. Excel calculates the total for the selected range.

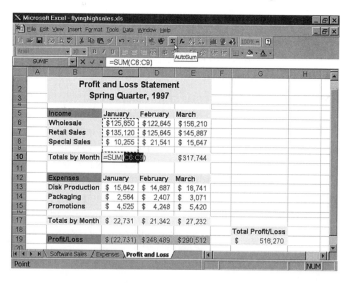

FIGURE 8.5 AutoSum inserts the SUM function and selects the cells it plans to total.

USING AUTOCALCULATE

When you wanted to quickly check a total in earlier versions of Excel, did you ever use a calculator or enter temporary formulas on a worksheet? If you did, you might find Excel's AutoCalculate feature very handy. AutoCalculate lets you quickly check a total or an average, count entries or numbers, and find the maximum or minimum number in a range.

Here's how AutoCalculate works. To check a total, select the range you want to sum. Excel automatically displays the answer in the AutoCalculate area (as shown in Figure 8.6). If you want to perform a different function on a range of numbers, select the range and right-click in the AutoCalculate area to display the shortcut menu. Then choose a function from the menu. For example, choose Count to count the numeric values in the range. The answer appears in the AutoCalculate area.

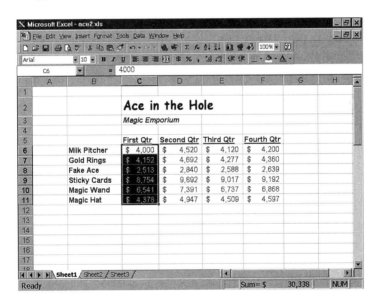

FIGURE 8.6 AutoCalculate lets you quickly view a sum.

USING THE FUNCTION WIZARD

Although you can type a function directly into a cell just as you can type formulas, you may find it easier to use the Function Wizard. The Function Wizard leads you through the process of inserting a function. The following steps walk you through using the Function Wizard:

1. Select the cell in which you want to insert the function. (You can insert a function by itself or as part of a formula.)

2. Type = or click the Edit Formula button on the Formula bar. The Formula Palette appears, as shown in Figure 8.7.

3. Select the function you want to insert from the Functions list by clicking the Functions button (see Figure 8.7). If you don't see your function listed, select More Functions at the bottom of the list.

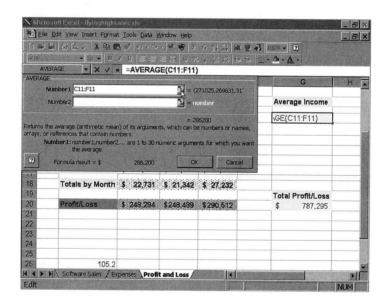

FIGURE 8.7   The Function Wizard helps you enter functions.

What's This Function?   If you don't know a lot about a particular function and you'd like to know more, click the Help button in the Formula Palette. When the Office Assistant appears, click Help with the Feature. Then click Help On Selected Function.

4. Enter the arguments for the formula. If you want to select a range of cells as an argument, click the Collapse Dialog button shown in Figure 8.7.

5. After selecting a range, click the Collapse Dialog button again to return to the Formula Palette.

6. Click OK. Excel inserts the function and argument in the selected cell and displays the result.

In this lesson, you learned how to use formulas in your worksheets and how to perform calculations with functions.

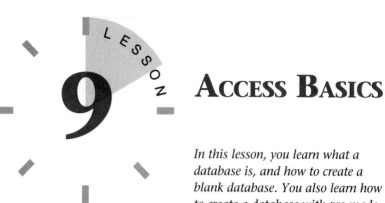

ACCESS BASICS

In this lesson, you learn what a database is, and how to create a blank database. You also learn how to create a database with pre-made tables, reports, and forms using the Database Wizard. In addition, you learn to save your database, close it, and reopen it.

ORIENTING YOURSELF WITH ACCESS

To launch the Access application, click the Start menu, Programs, Microsoft Access. When you start Access, the first thing you see is a dialog box prompting you to create a new database or open an existing one (see Figure 9.1). For now, click Cancel.

FIGURE 9.1 This Microsoft Access dialog box appears each time you start Access.

Access is much like any other Windows program—it contains menus, toolbars, a status bar, and so on. Figure 9.2 points out these landmarks. Notice that in Figure 9.2, many of the toolbar buttons are grayed out (which means you can't use them right now). There's also nothing in the work area. That's because no database file is open. As you will see, the Access screen becomes a much busier place in later lessons when you begin working with a database. The buttons will become available, and your database will appear in the work area.

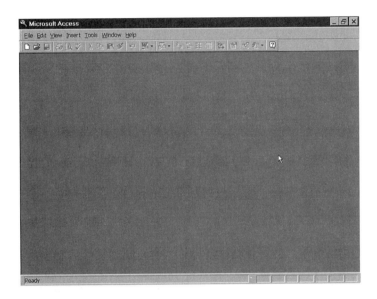

FIGURE 9.2 Access has the same interface landmarks as any Windows program.

UNDERSTANDING DATABASES

Strictly speaking, a database is any collection of information. Your local telephone book, for example, is a database, as is your Rolodex file and the card catalog at your local library. With a computerized database in Microsoft Access, you can store information as these three examples do, but you can also do much more. For instance, if you keep a list of all your business customers in an Access database, you can:

- Print out a list of all customers who haven't bought anything in the last 60 days, along with their phone numbers, so you can call each one.

- Sort the customers by ZIP code and print out mailing labels in that order. (Some bulk-mailing services require you to presort by ZIP code to get the cheaper mailing rate.)

- Create a simple on-screen order entry form that even your most technically unskilled employee can use successfully.

These examples only scratch the surface of what you can do. With Access, you can manipulate your data in almost any way you can dream.

Tables are the central focus of all activities; reports summarize and organize the table data; forms help you enter information into the table; queries help you find information you want to use in the table. Each of these elements are described in the sections that follow.

TABLES

The heart of each database is its tables. A table is a lot like a spreadsheet. Figure 9.3 shows a data table (or just table for short).

Access stores each database entry (such as each client or each inventory item) in its own row; this is a record. For example, all the information about White Clover Markets, including the Address, City, State, and Zip code, forms a single record (see Figure 9.3).

Each type of detail is kept in its own column—a field. For example, Client ID is one field, and Company Name is another. All the company names in the entire table are collectively known as the Company Name field.

At the intersection of a field and a row is the individual bit of data for that particular record; this area is a *cell*. For example, in the cell where the City column and the White Clover Markets record intersect, you find Seattle.

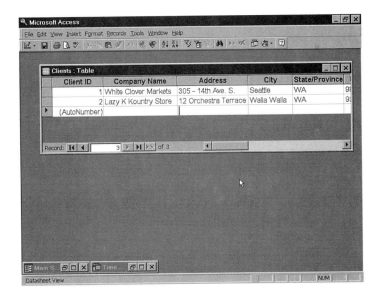

FIGURE 9.3 A typical table in Access.

You learn how to create tables in Lesson 10, "Working with Tables." Each database file can have many tables. For instance, you might have one table that lists all your customers and another table that lists information about the products you sell. A third table might keep track of your salespeople and their performance.

FORMS

All the data you enter into your database ends up in a table for storage. You can enter information directly into a table, but it's a little awkward to do so. Most people find it easier to create a special on-screen form in which to enter the data. A form resembles any fill-in-the-blanks sheet that you might complete by hand, such as a job application.

Access links the form to the table and stores the information you put into the form in the table. For instance, take a look at Figure 9.4. Access stores the client data entered on this form in the table shown in Figure 9.3.

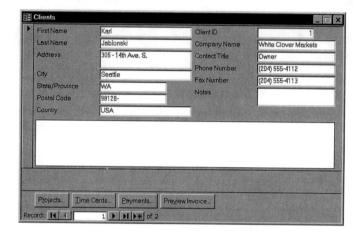

FIGURE 9.4 Forms make data entry more convenient.

REPORTS

While forms are designed to be used on-screen, reports are designed to be printed. Reports are specially formatted collections of data, organized according to your specifications. For instance, you might want to create a report of all your clients like the one shown in Figure 9.5.

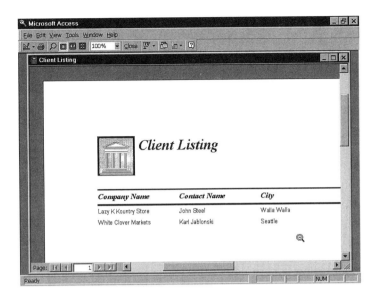

FIGURE 9.5   You might print this report to distribute to other employees.

QUERIES

A query provides you with a way of weeding out the information you don't want to see, so that you can more clearly see the information you do need. You can think of it as a sieve into which you dump your data: the data you don't want falls through the holes in the sieve, leaving only the data in which you're interested.

CHOOSING HOW YOU CREATE YOUR DATABASE

When you create a database, you are really creating a database file. This file holds everything you create for a database—not only all the data, but also the customized forms, reports, and indexes.

Before you create your database, you have an important decision to make. Should you create a blank database from scratch, and then manually create all the tables, reports, and forms you'll need? Or should you use a Database Wizard, which does all that for you?

Database Wizard Access comes with several Database Wizards. These are mini-programs that question you about your needs and then create a database structure that matches them. (You will enter the actual data yourself.)

The answer depends on how well the available wizards match your needs. If there is a Database Wizard that is close to what you want, it's quickest to use it to create your database, and then modify it as needed. If you're in a hurry, using a wizard can save you lots of time.

On the other hand, if you want a special-purpose database that isn't similar to any of the wizards, or if you're creating the database primarily as a training exercise for yourself, you should create the blank database.

CREATING A BLANK DATABASE

Creating a blank database is simple because you're just creating an outer shell at this point, without any tables, forms, and so on. This section outlines two ways to do that.

If you just started Access, and the Microsoft Access dialog box is still displayed, click Blank Database and then the OK button (see Figure 9.6).

FIGURE 9.6 When you first start Access, you can start a new database quickly from the Microsoft Access dialog box.

If the dialog box is gone, you can't get it back until you exit from Access and restart it. But you don't need that dialog box to start a new database. At any time you can follow these steps:

1. Select File, New or click the New button on the toolbar. The New dialog box appears (see Figure 9.7).

2. Click the General tab, if necessary, to bring it to the top. Then double-click the Blank Database icon, and the File New Database dialog box appears.

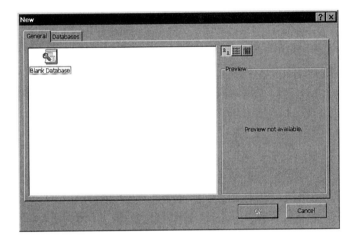

FIGURE 9.7 The New dialog box's different tabs give you options to create different kinds of databases.

3. Type a name for your new database (preferably something descriptive) in the File Name box. For example, I typed "Kennel Records." Then click Create. Access creates the new database, as shown in Figure 9.8.

Your database is completely blank at this point. You can click any of the tabs in the database window (see Figure 9.8), but you won't find anything listed on any of them.

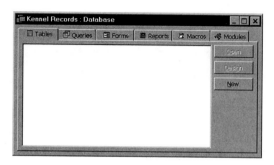

FIGURE 9.8   A new, blank database window.

CREATING A DATABASE WITH DATABASE WIZARD

A Database Wizard can create almost all the tables, forms, and reports you will ever need, automatically. The trick is choosing the right wizard to suit your purpose. Follow these steps:

1. If you just started Access, and the Microsoft Access dialog box is still on-screen, click Database Wizard and click OK. Or, if you've already closed the dialog box, select File, New Database. Either way, the New dialog box appears.

2. Click the Databases tab to display the list of wizards.

3. Click one of the Database Wizards (they're the icons with the magic wands across them). For this example, choose Contact Management. A preview appears in the Preview area.

4. When you've found the wizard you want, click OK. The File New Database dialog box appears.

5. Type a name for the database and click Create to continue. The wizard starts, and some information appears explaining what the wizard will do.

6. Click Next to continue. A list of the tables to be created appears (see Figure 9.9). The tables appear on the left, and the selected table's fields on the right.

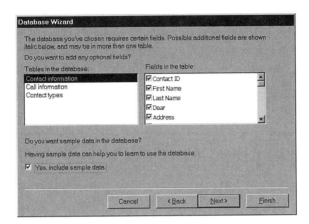

FIGURE 9.9   These are the tables and fields that this wizard creates automatically for you.

7. Click a table and examine its list of fields. Optional fields are in italic. To include an optional field, click it to place a check mark next to it.

I Don't Want These Tables and Fields!   Sorry, that's the price you pay for going with a prefabricated wizard. You can't deselect any fields except the optional (italicized) ones. But you can delete the tables and fields you don't want later. If the tables and fields seem to be totally inappropriate, perhaps you are using the wrong wizard for your needs. If so, click Cancel and try another.

8. (Optional) If you are creating this database for a learning experience only, click the Yes, Include Sample Data check box. This tells Access to enter some dummy records into the database so you can see how they will work in the database.

9. Click Next to continue. The wizard asks you what kind of screen display style you want.

10. Click a display style in the list and examine the preview of that style that appears. When you have decided on a style, click it and click Next. The wizard asks you for a style for printed reports.

11. Click a report style and examine the preview of it. When you have decided on a style, click it and click Next.

12. The wizard asks what title you want for the database. The title will appear on reports, and it can be different from the filename. Enter a title (see Figure 9.10).

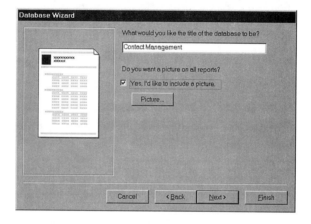

FIGURE 9.10   Enter a title for the database and choose a graphic to use for a logo (if you want).

13. (Optional) If you want to include a picture (such as your company logo) on your forms and reports, click the Yes, I'd Like to Include a Picture check box. Then click the Picture button, choose a graphics file (change the drive and/or folder if needed), and click Open to return to the wizard.

14. Click Next to continue. When you get to the Finish screen, click Finish. The wizard goes to work creating your database. (It may take several minutes.)

When the database is finished, the Main Switchboard window
appears (see Figure 9.11). The Switchboard opens automatically
whenever you open the database.

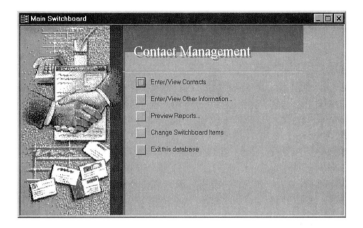

FIGURE 9.11 The Switchboard window is a bonus provided by
the Database Wizards.

All the databases created by a Database Wizard include the Main
Switchboard. The Main Switchboard is nothing more than a fancy
form with some programming built in. It lets you perform common tasks with the database by clicking a button. We won't be
working with the Main Switchboard, so click the Main Switchboard window's Close (X) button to get rid of it.

Once you close the Switchboard window, you'll see the database
window. If it's minimized, double-click its title bar (bottom left
corner of the screen) to open it again. Click the Tables tab, and
you see that several tables have been created for you. Click the
other tabs to see the other objects created as well.

SAVING A DATABASE

You need to save your work so that you don't lose anything
you've typed after you turn off the computer. When you created

the database, you saved it by naming it. When you enter each record, Access automatically saves your work.

When you change the structure of a table, form, or other object, however, Access will not let you close that object or close the database without confirming whether or not you want to save your changes. You'll see a dialog box asking you to click Yes to save your changes.

Notice that the Save and Save As commands on the File menu aren't even available most of the time; they're grayed out. When you have a particular object (such as a table) highlighted in the Database window, the Save As/Export command is available. You can use this command to save your table in a different format that another program (such as Excel) can read.

 Using Tables in Other Programs   Another way to copy a table to another application or another database is with the Copy and Paste commands. High-light the table in the Database window and select Edit, Copy. Then open a different database or application and select Edit, Paste. A dialog box opens, giving you the options of pasting the table structure only or the structure and the data. You can also choose to append the data to an existing table, if the fields match up.

Closing a Database

When you finish working with a database, you should close it. When you are finished using Access, exiting the program will close the database along with the program.

But, what if you're not ready to close Access? If you want to close one database and then open another, close the database by selecting File, Close.

Can't I Have More Than One Database Open? Sure you can. In fact, you might want several open so that you can transfer data between them. However, if your computer is short on memory (less than 16 megabytes), you'll want to close all files you're not using so Access will run faster.

OPENING A DATABASE

You won't always want to create a *new* database from scratch as you did in the previous sections, you'll open your existing one.

The easiest way to open a database you've recently used is to select it from the File menu. Follow these steps:

1. Open the File menu. At the bottom of the menu, Access lists up to four databases you've recently used.

2. Click the database you want to open.

If the database you want to open isn't listed, you'll need to use select File, Open or click the Open button on the Standard toolbar. The Open dialog box appears (see Figure 9.12).

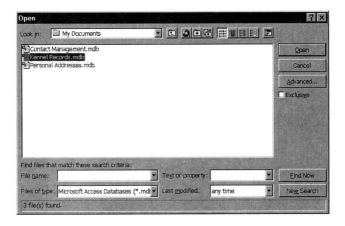

FIGURE 9.12   Open a different database file with this dialog box.

If the file isn't in the currently displayed folder, change drives and folders as necessary, and double-click the file to open it.

In this lesson, you learned what a database is, and how to create a blank database. You also learned how to create a database with pre-made tables, reports, and forms using the Database Wizard. In addition, you learned to save your database, close it, and reopen it.

WORKING WITH TABLES

In this lesson, you learn about designing tables and normalization. You also learn how to create a table in three different ways.

DETERMINING WHAT TABLES YOU NEED

How many tables will you need? Technically, you will need only one. That's the minimum with which a database can function. However, the biggest mistake most people make with Access is to put too much information in one table. Access is a relational database program; unlike more simple database programs, it's meant to handle lots of tables and create relationships among them. Figure 10.1 shows a list of tables in a database that keeps track of the employee hours spent on various projects.

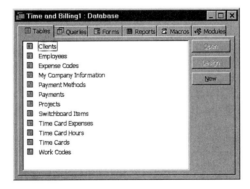

FIGURE 10.1 Access really shines when you take advantage of its capability to store many tables.

Plan Tables Now! You should plan your tables before you create your database because changing a table's structure after it has been filled with data is difficult.

NORMALIZING YOUR DATABASE

When a database suffers from poor table organization, experts say it's not normalized. There are rules that govern how a relational database should store its tables. Those rules are called the rules of *Data Normalization*. Data Normalization is the process of making tables as efficient and compact as possible to eliminate the possibility for confusion and error.

There are five normalization rules, but the latter ones are fairly complicated and are used mostly by database professionals. In this lesson, I explain the first two normalization rules, which are all a beginner really needs to understand in order to avoid major mistakes.

RULE #1: AVOID REPEATED INFORMATION

You might want to keep contact information on your customers along with a record of each transaction they make. If you kept it all in one table (like the one shown in the preceding figure), you would have to repeat the customer's full name, address, and phone number each time you entered a new transaction!. It would also be a nightmare if the customer's address changed; you would have to make the change to every transaction.

A better way is to assign each customer an ID number. Include that ID number in a table that contains names and addresses. Then you can include the same ID number as a link in a separate table that contains transactions.

RULE #2: AVOID REDUNDANT DATA

You might want to keep track of which employees have attended certain training classes. There are lots of employees and lots of classes. One way to do this would be to keep it all in a single Personnel table, as follows.

But what if an employee takes more than one class? You would have to add a duplicate line in the table to list it, and then you would have the problem described in the previous section—multiple records with virtually identical field entries. And what if the only employee who has taken a certain class leaves the company? When you delete that employee's record, you delete the information about the credit hours, too.

A better way would be to create separate tables for Employees, Classes, and Training.

DESIGNING YOUR TABLES

Don't be overwhelmed by all this information about database normalization. Good table organization boils down to a few simple principles:

- Each table should have a theme.

- If you see that you might end up repeating data in a table in the future, plan now to separate the information that will be repeated into its own table.

- If there is a list of reference information you want to preserve, put it in its own table.

- Wherever possible, use ID numbers, as they help you link tables together later and help you avoid typing errors that come from entering long text strings over and over.

CREATING A TABLE USING THE TABLE WIZARD

When you create a table, you can create it from *scratch*, or you can use the Table Wizard. The Table Wizard can save you lots of time by creating and formatting all the right fields for a certain purpose.

Access comes with dozens of pre-made business and personal tables from which to choose. You can pick and choose among all the fields in all the pre-made tables, constructing a table that's right for your needs. Even if you can't find all the fields you need in pre-made tables, you may want to use the Table Wizard to save time and then add the missing fields later.

There are three Table Wizards—the standard Table Wizard, the Import Table Wizard, and the Link Table Wizard. In this lesson, you'll be working with only the standard Table Wizard.

To create a table using the Table Wizard, follow these steps:

1. Select Insert, Table from the menu bar along the top of the screen. Or in the Database window, click the Tables tab and click New. The New Table dialog box appears (see Figure 10.2).

Figure 10.2   Indicate how you want to create the new table.

2. Click Table Wizard and click OK. The Table Wizard window appears (see Figure 10.3).

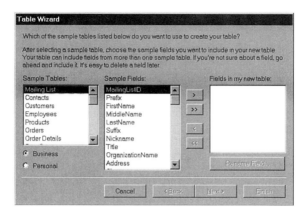

Figure 10.3   Choose your table's fields from those that come with any of the pre-made tables.

3. Click a table in the Sample Tables list. Access then displays its fields in the Sample Fields list.

4. If you see a field that you want to include in your new table, select it in the Sample Fields list; then click the > button to move it to the Fields in My New Table list. To move the entire contents of the selected Sample Table to your list, click the >> button.

Name Change!   If you see a field that is close to what you want, but you prefer a different name for it, first add it to your list (as described in steps 3 and 4). Then click the field name to select it, click the Rename Field button, type a new name, and click OK. This renames the field on your list only—not on the original.

5. Repeat steps 3 and 4 to select other fields from other sample tables until the list of fields in your new table is complete. (You can remove a field from the list by clicking the < button, and you can remove all the fields and start over by clicking the << button.) When you're finished adding fields, click Next to continue.

6. Next the wizard asks for a name for the table. Type a more descriptive name to replace the default one.

7. Click Yes, Set A Primary Key For Me to have the wizard choose your primary key field, or No, I'll Set The Primary Key to do it yourself. If you choose Yes, then click Next. Primary keys are explained in the section "Setting the Primary Key."

8. A dialog box appears (see Figure 10.4) asking which field will be the primary key. Open the drop-down list and select the field.

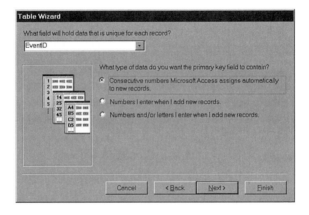

Figure 10.4   You can set your own primary key for the table.

9. Choose a data type for the primary key field (data types are explained in the section "Understanding Data Types and Formats"). For now, just choose Consecutive Numbers. Click Next to continue.

10. If you already have at least one table in this database, a screen appears asking about the relationship between tables. Just click Next to move past it for now.

11. At the Finish screen, click one of the following options:

    • Modify the table design. This takes you into Table Design view, the same as if you had created all those fields yourself. Choose this if you have some changes you want to make to the table before you use it.

- Enter data directly into the table. This takes you to Table Datasheet view, where you can enter records into the rows of the table. Choose this if the table's design seems perfect to you as-is.

- Enter data into the table using a form the Wizard creates for me.

12. Click Finish, and you're taken to the area of Access that you indicated you wanted to go (in step 11).

If you decide you don't want to work with this table anymore for now (no matter what you selected in step 11), click the Close (X) button for the window that appears.

Now you have a table. In the Database window, when you click the Tables tab, you can see your table in the list (see Figure 10.5).

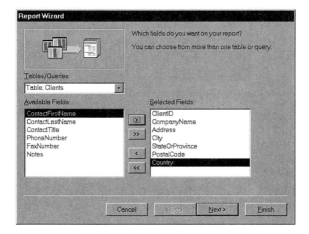

Figure 10.5   Now you have a table on your Tables tab.

CREATING A TABLE IN TABLE DESIGN VIEW

Access's wizards are very useful, but they do not offer the flexibility you have when performing the equivalent tasks from scratch. For instance, if you want to create a table that contains special fields not available in a wizard, you are better off creating that table in Table Design view.

To create a table in Table Design view, follow these steps:

1. Select Insert, Table or, from the Database window, click the Table tab and click the New button. The New Table dialog box appears (see Figure 10.6).

FIGURE 10.6 Start your new table in Design view.

 Quick! A New Object! Instead of step 1, you can click the New Object drop-down arrow on the toolbar. A drop-down list appears, showing the available object types. Select New Table from that list.

2. Click Design View and click OK. Table Design view opens (see Figure 10.7).

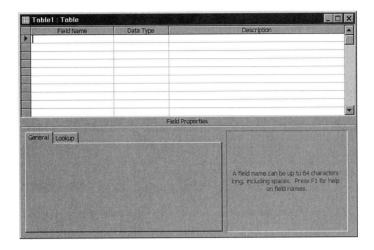

FIGURE 10.7   From Table Design view, you can control the entire table creation process.

3. Type a field name on the first empty line in the Field Name column; then press Tab to move to the Data Type column.

 Field Naming Rules   Field names—and all other objects in Access for that matter—can contain up to 64 characters and can include spaces and any symbols except periods (.), exclamation marks (!), accent grave symbols ('), or square brackets ([]). However, you may want to stick with short, easy-to-remember names.

4. When you move to the Data Type column, an arrow appears there for a drop-down list. Open the Data Type drop-down list and select a field type. (See the section "Understanding Data Types and Formats" later in this lesson if you need help deciding which field type to use.)

5. (Optional) Press Tab to move to the Description column, and then type a description of the field. (The table will work fine even without a description.)

6. In the bottom half of the dialog box, you see Field Properties for the field type you selected (see Figure 10.8). Make any changes desired to them.

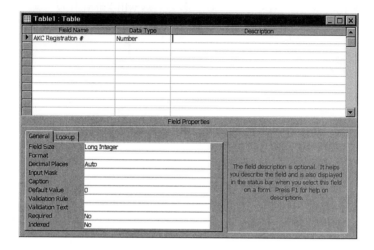

Figure 10.8   The Field Properties change depending on the field type.

7. If you have more fields to enter, repeat steps 3–6.

8. Click the Table Design window's Close (X) button.

9. When you are asked if you want to save your changes to the table, click Yes. The Save As dialog box appears.

10. Type a name for the table in the Table Name text box and click OK.

 No Primary Key!   When you close Table Design view, you may get a message that no primary key has been assigned. See the section "Setting the Primary Key" later in this lesson to learn what to do.

UNDERSTANDING DATA TYPES AND FORMATS

Each field must have a type so that Access will know how to handle its contents. Here are the types you can choose from:

Text   Plain, ordinary typed text, which can include numbers, letters, and symbols. A Text field can contain up to 255 characters.

Memo   More plain, ordinary text, except this one doesn't have a maximum field length. So you can type an almost infinite amount of text (64,000 characters).

Number   A plain, ordinary number (not a currency value or a date). Access won't allow any text in a Number field.

Date/Time   Just that—a date or a time.

Currency   A number formatted as an amount of money.

AutoNumber   A number that Access automatically fills in for each consecutive record.

Yes/No   The answer to a true/false question. It can contain either of two values, which might be Yes or No, True or False, On or Off.

OLE Object   A link to another database or file. This is an advanced feature that I don't cover in this book.

Hyperlink   A link to a location on the World Wide Web.

Lookup Wizard   Lets you create a list to choose a value from another table or list of values in a combo box for each record. It is another advanced feature that I won't cover here.

In addition to a field type, each field has formatting options you can set. They appear in the bottom half of the dialog box in the Field Properties area. The formatting options change depending on the field type, and there are too many to list here. But these are some of the most important ones you'll encounter:

Field Size   The maximum number of characters a user can input in that field.

Format   A drop-down list of the available formats for that field type. You can also create custom formats.

Default Value   If a field is usually going to contain a certain value (for instance, a certain zip code for almost everyone), you can enter it here to save time. It will always appear in a new record, and you can type over it in the rare instances when it doesn't apply.

Decimal Places   For number fields, you can set the default number of decimal places so a number will show.

Required   Choose yes or no to tell Access whether a user should be allowed to leave this field blank when entering a new record.

SETTING THE PRIMARY KEY

Every table must have at least one field that has a unique value for each record. For instance, in a table of the dogs your kennel owns, you might assign an ID number to each dog, and have an ID # field in your table. Or you might choose to use each dog's AKC (American Kennel Club) registration number. This unique identifier field is known as the *primary key* field.

You must tell Access which field you are going to use as the primary key so that it can prevent you from accidentally entering the same value for more than one record in that field. To set a primary key, follow these steps:

1. In Table Design view, select the field that you want to use for the primary key.

2. Select Edit, Primary Key or click the Primary Key button on the toolbar. A key symbol appears to the left of the field name, as shown in Figure 10.9.

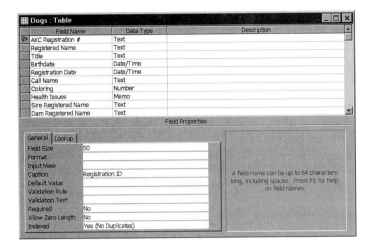

FIGURE 10.9   The primary key field is marked by a key symbol.

SWITCHING BETWEEN DESIGN AND DATASHEET VIEWS

When working with tables, you can use one of two available views—Design view or Datasheet view.

One easy way to switch between the views is to click the View drop-down arrow on the toolbar (it's the leftmost button); then select the view you want from the drop-down list that appears.

Another way to switch between views is to open the View menu and select Table Design or Datasheet, depending on which view you are currently in. If you're moving from Table Design view to Datasheet view, you may be asked to save your work. If so, click Yes. If you're asked for a name for the table, type one and click OK.

CREATING A TABLE IN DATASHEET VIEW

Some people prefer to create a table in Datasheet view. However, Access designed Datasheet view for data entry and viewing, not for table structure changes. I do not recommend creating the table this way, because you do not have access to as many controls as you do with Table Design view.

To create a table in Datasheet view, follow these steps:

1. Select Insert, Table.

2. Click Datasheet View and click OK. A blank table opens, as shown in Figure 10.10.

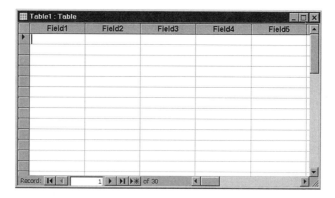

FIGURE 10.10   Creating a new table in Datasheet view gives you a quick, generic table.

How Do I Set the Field Names?   When you create a table in Datasheet view, the fields have generic names such as Field1. To change a field name, click the present name to select the column. Then select Format, Rename Column, type the new name, and press Enter.

3. Make any necessary changes to the design of the table. When you finish making changes, click the table's Close (X) button. Access asks if you want to save the design changes. Click Yes. When Access asks for a name for the table, type one and click OK.

EDITING FIELDS AND THEIR PROPERTIES

No matter how you create your table (whether with or without the Table Wizard), you can modify it using Table Design view. If you create the table without Table Wizard, Table Design view will look very familiar to you.

From the Database window, click the Table tab, select the table you want to work with, and click the Design button. Once you're in Table Design view (see Figure 10.11), you can edit any field. Here is the general procedure:

1. Click any field name in the Field Name list.

2. If desired, click the field's Data Type area and select a new data type from the drop-down list.

3. In the Field Properties area (the bottom half of the Table Design screen), click any text box in order to change its value. Some text boxes have drop-down lists, which you can activate by clicking in the box.

4. Repeat steps 1–3 for each field you want to change.

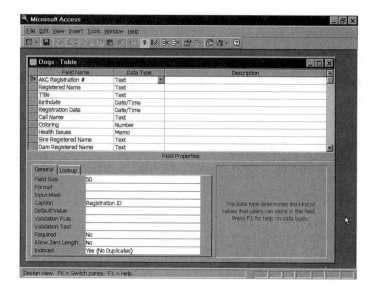

FIGURE 10.11   In Table Design view, you can modify the attributes of any field.

ADDING FIELDS

Before you enter data into your table, you should make very sure that you have included all the fields you'll need. Why? Because if you add a field later, you'll have to go back and enter a value in that field for each record that you've already entered. In addition, if you change the field length, you risk truncating or invalidating data that's already been entered.

You can add a field in either Table Design view or Datasheet view. Try it in Table Design view first:

1. Select the field before which you want the new field to appear.

2. Click the Insert Rows button on the toolbar or select Insert, Row. A blank row appears in the Field Name list.

3. Enter a name, type, description, and so on for the new field.

DELETING FIELDS

If you realize that you don't need one or more fields that you've created, now is the time to get rid of them. Otherwise, you'll needlessly enter information into each record that you will never use.

You can erase fields in either Table Design view or Datasheet view. To delete a field in Table Design view, switch to Table Design view (if you're not already there). Select a field and press the Delete key on your keyboard.

If you prefer, you can delete the field in Datasheet view. Whereas there's an advantage to using Table Design view to add fields, there's no significant difference when you delete fields. You can accomplish a field deletion easily in either view. To delete a field in Datasheet view switch to Datasheet view (if you're not already there) and select the entire column for the field you want to delete. Select Edit, Delete Column.

DELETING A TABLE

Now that you've created a table and worked with it a bit, you may discover that you made so many mistakes creating it that it would be easier to start over. Or you may have several tables by now, and you might decide that you don't need all of them. Whatever the reason, it's easy to delete a table. Follow these steps:

1. From the Database window, click the Tables tab. Select the table you want to delete.

2. Select Edit, Delete or press the Delete key on your keyboard. A message appears asking if you are sure you want to do this. Click Yes.

In this lesson, you learned about designing tables and normalization. You also learn how to create a table in three different ways.

11

LESSON

WORKING WITH DATA AND RELATIONSHIPS

In this lesson, you learn how to work with data and how to link two or more tables together so you can work with them as you would a single table.

ENTERING A RECORD

At this point, you have created your table structure and you've fine-tuned it with the settings you want. It's finally time to enter records. Open the table and follow these steps to enter a record:

1. Click in the first empty cell in the first empty column.

2. Type the value for that field and press Tab to move to the next field, and then type its value. Continue pressing Tab until you get to the last field.

3. When you press Tab in the last field, the insertion point moves to the first field in the next line, where you can start a new record.

4. Continue entering records until you've filled them all.

> **Printing a Table** Sometimes you may want a quick printout of the raw data in the table. In that case, open the table and click the Print button on the Standard toolbar. Access prints the table.

Changing a Cell's Content

Editing a cell's content is easy. You can either replace the old content completely or edit it. Which is better? It depends on how much you need to change; you make the call.

If the old content is completely wrong, it's best to enter new data from scratch. To replace the old content in a field, follow these steps:

1. Select the cell whose contents you want to replace. Do this by clicking it or by moving to it with the keyboard.
2. Type the new data. The new data replaces the old data.

If you need to make a small change to a cell's content, there's no reason to completely retype it. Instead, edit the content. Follow these steps to learn how:

1. Position the mouse pointer in the cell so the mouse pointer looks like an I-beam (see Figure 11.1).
2. Click once, and an insertion point appears in the cell.

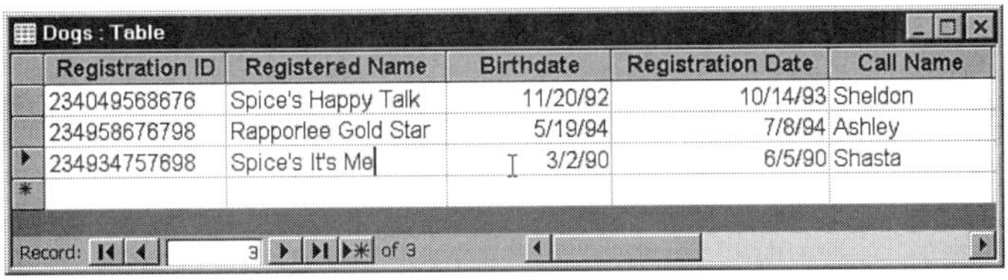

FIGURE 11.1 Click in a cell to place the insertion point in it.

3. Use the arrow keys to move the insertion point to the location in the cell where you want to start editing.
4. Press Backspace to remove the character to the left of the insertion point, or press Delete to remove the character to the right of it. Then type your change.

SELECTING RECORDS

In addition to editing individual cells in a record, you may want to work with an entire record. To do this, click in the gray square to the left of the record (the record selection area). Access highlights the entire record—displaying white letters on black—as shown in Figure 11.2.

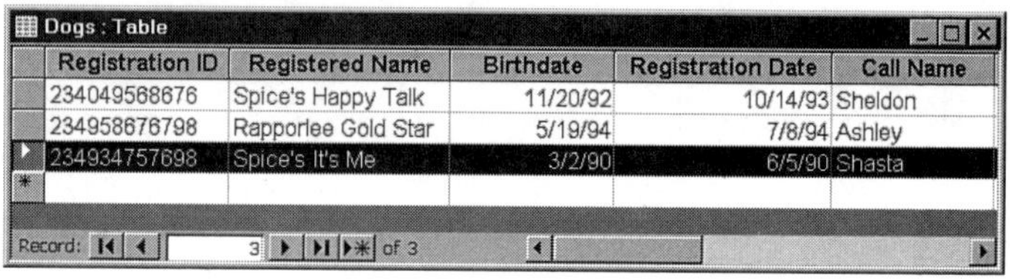

⊞ Dogs : Table				_□×
Registration ID	Registered Name	Birthdate	Registration Date	Call Name
234049568876	Spice's Happy Talk	11/20/92	10/14/93	Sheldon
234958676798	Rapporlee Gold Star	5/19/94	7/8/94	Ashley
▶ 234934757698	Spice's It's Me	3/2/90	6/5/90	Shasta
*				

Record: I◀ ◀ 3 ▶ ▶I ▶* of 3

FIGURE 11.2   The selected record.

You might want to select several records as a group to perform an action on all of them at once. To do so, select the first record, press and hold down Shift, and select the other records. You can select only adjacent groups of records; you can't pick them from all over the list.

INSERTING NEW RECORDS

Access inserts new records automatically. When you start to type a record, a new line appears below it, waiting for another record (as you see in Figure 10.3). You can't insert new records between existing ones. You must always insert new records at the end of the table.

What If I Want the Records in a Different Order?   It's easy to sort your records to put them in any order you want. You learn how to sort later in the section "Sorting Data."

DELETING RECORDS

If you find that one or more records is outdated or doesn't belong in the table, you can easily delete it. You can even delete several records at a time. Simply select the record(s) you want to delete and press the Delete key on the keyboard.

Delete versus Delete Record If you select the entire record, there's no difference between these two commands. However, if you select only a portion of the record there is a difference: Delete removes only the selected text, while Delete Record removes the entire record. You cannot undo a deletion, so be careful what you delete.

MOVING AND COPYING DATA

As with any Windows program, you can use the Cut, Copy, and Paste commands to copy and move data. Follow these steps:

1. Select the field(s), record(s), cell(s), or text that you want to move or copy.

2. Open the Edit menu and select Cut (to move) or Copy (to copy). Or, click the Cut or Copy button on the Standard toolbar.

3. Position the insertion point where you want to insert the cut or copied material.

4. Select Edit, Paste or click the Paste button on the Standard toolbar. Access places the cut or copied material in that location.

Moving and Copying You can move and copy entire objects—not just individual fields and records. From the Database window, select the table, report, or query that you want to move or copy. Then execute the Cut or Copy command, move to where you want the object to go (for example, in a different database), and execute the Paste command.

SORTING DATA

Although you enter your records into the database in some sort of logical order, at some point, you will want them in a different order. For instance, we might enter the dogs in our kennel according to registration number, but later we might want to look at the list in order of the dogs' birth dates, from oldest to youngest.

The Sort command is the perfect solution to this problem. With Sort, you can rearrange the records according to any field you like. You can sort in either ascending order (A to Z and 1 to 10) or descending order (Z to A and 10 to 1).

Follow these steps to sort records:

1. Click anywhere in the field by which you want to sort.

2. Click the Sort Ascending button or the Sort Descending button on the toolbar. Or if you prefer, select Records, Sort, and then choose Ascending or Descending from the submenu. Figure 11.3 shows our table of dogs sorted in Ascending order by birth date.

Registration ID	Registered Name	Title	Birthdate	Registration Date	Call Name
304958678808	Wempen's Best	None	8/18/85	8/25/85	Buddy
234934757698	Spice's It's Me	UD	3/2/90	6/5/90	Shasta
304959686928	Spice's Krazy 4 U	UDX	4/9/90	4/9/90	Betsy Mae
304958698273	Spice's Never More	CH	4/9/90	4/9/90	Cindy
304958879827	Spice's Sure Thing	CH	4/9/90	6/2/90	Carly
304958602938	Princess of the Ring	None	8/12/91	8/15/91	Bubbles
294850928374	Princess Bride	None	11/20/92	10/14/93	Loudmouth
234049568676	Spice's Happy Talk	None	11/20/92	10/14/93	Sheldon
304956820394	King of the Hill	CD	2/3/94	5/6/94	Champ
203948657698	Happiglade Tornado	UD	2/3/94	5/6/94	Ruby
234958676798	Rapporlee Gold Star	CDX	5/19/94	7/8/94	Ashley
203948576987	Carrolton Make a Wish	CD	9/12/95	10/15/95	Shelby
230495869287	Brazen Puppy Gold	None	3/3/96	5/6/96	Boopsie

Record: 4 of 13

FIGURE 11.3 Access sorted this table in Ascending order by the Birthdate column.

3. If you want to restore the records to their presorted order, select Records, Remove Filter/Sort.

 Presorted Order   If you defined a Primary Key field when you created your database, the records appear sorted in ascending order according to that field by default. This is the order they revert to when you remove a sort (as in step 3). If you save the datasheet or form without removing the sort, the sort order becomes part of that object.

UNDERSTANDING RELATIONSHIPS

Relationships can be extremely complicated and thorny. I'm showing you only simple examples in this lesson because that's probably all you need as a casual user.

The following example should illustrate relationships more clearly. Say I have two tables containing information about my customers. One table, called Customers, contains their names and addresses; the other, called Orders, contains their orders. The two tables would have a common field—Customer ID#. All records in the Orders table would correspond to a record in the Customers table because you must be a customer to place an order. (This is called a one-to-many relationship because one customer could have many orders.)

CREATING A RELATIONSHIP BETWEEN TABLES

To create a relationship between tables, you open the Relationships window and add relationships from there. Follow these steps:

1. From anywhere in the database select Tools, Relationships.

2. If you have not selected any tables yet, the Show Table dialog box (shown in Figure 11.4) appears automatically.

If it doesn't, open the Relationships menu and select
Show Table or click the Show Table toolbar button.

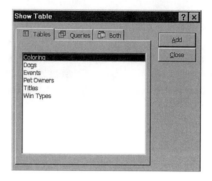

FIGURE 11.4   Add tables to your Relationships window.

3. Click a table that you want to use for a relationship, and
   then click the Add button.

4. Repeat step 3 until you have selected all the tables with
   which you want to work. When you're finished, click
   Close. Each table appears in its own box in the Relationships window, as shown in Figure 11.5.

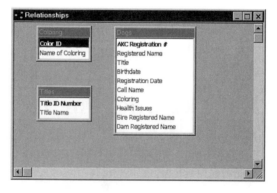

FIGURE 11.5   I added three tables to my Relationships window.

5. Click a field in one table that you want to link to another
   table.

6. Hold down the mouse button and drag away from the se-
    lected field. Your mouse pointer will turn into a little rect-
    angle. Drop the little rectangle onto the destination field.
    The Relationships dialog box appears (see Figure 11.6).

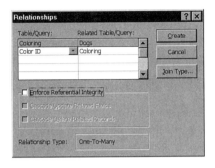

FIGURE 11.6   The Relationships dialog box asks you to define
the relationship you're creating.

7. Choose any Referential Integrity options you want (see
    the following section "Understanding Referential Integ-
    rity"), and then click Create. If all goes well, a relation-
    ship is created, and you see a line between the two fields
    in the Relationships window (see Figure 11.7).

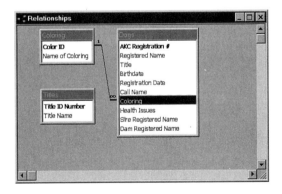

FIGURE 11.7   The line represents a relationship between the two
fields.

Understanding Referential Integrity

Referential Integrity keeps you from making data entry mistakes. It says, essentially, that all the information in the two fields should match. If there is an entry in one table in the linked field that doesn't exist in the other, it's a problem that Referential Integrity corrects.

An example will make this clearer. In the Coloring field in my Dogs database, I have a number that matches up with the Color ID field in the Coloring table. The Coloring table lists all the allowable colors for the breed of dog. I don't want my clerks to be able to accidentally enter a number in the Dogs table that doesn't match up with one of the colors in the Coloring table, so I chose to Enforce Referential Integrity. Now Access won't let anyone enter anything in the Coloring field of the Dogs table (the many or infinity side) except one of the numbers contained in the Color ID field in the Coloring table (the one side).

What happens if someone tries? It depends on which of the other two check boxes shown in Figure 11.6 were marked.

Here is a summary of the check boxes and their functions:

- Neither Marked   Access gives an error message that you need a related record in the "[Table Name]" and will not allow you to make the entry.

- Cascade Update Related Fields   If this check box is marked and you make a change to the related table (in our example, the Coloring table), the change will be made in the other table (the Dogs table) as well. For instance, if I decided to change a certain coloring number from 7 to 8, and I made the change in the Coloring table (the one side), all the 7s in the Dogs table (the many side) would change to 8s.

- Cascade Delete Related Fields   If this check box is marked and you make a change to the one table (for instance, Coloring) so that the entries in the related table aren't valid anymore, Access deletes the entries in the related table. For instance, if I deleted the record in the Coloring table for Coloring ID number 3, all the dogs from my Dogs table that had coloring number 3 would also be deleted.

The first time you try to use Referential Integrity, you will likely get an error message because there is usually some condition that prevents it from working. For instance, when I first created the relationship shown in Figure 11.7 with Enforce Referential Integrity marked, Access would not allow it because the field type for the Coloring field in the Dogs table was set to Text while the Color ID field in the Coloring table was a number. (It didn't matter that I had entered only numbers in the Coloring field in the Dogs table.)

EDITING A RELATIONSHIP

After a relationship is created, you can edit it by redisplaying the Relationships dialog box (refer to Figure 11.6). To do so, double-click the relationship's line. From there, you can edit the relationship using the same controls you did when you created it.

REMOVING A RELATIONSHIP

To delete a relationship, just click it in the Relationships window and press the Delete key. Access will ask for confirmation. Click Yes, and the relationship disappears.

In this lesson, you learn how to work with data and how to link two or more tables together so you can work with them as you would a single table.

WORKING WITH QUERIES

In this lesson, you learn how a query can help you find the information you need, how to create a simple query using the Simple Query Wizard, and how to modify and strengthen your queries.

UNDERSTANDING QUERIES

Access offers many ways to help you narrow down the information you're looking at, including sorting and filtering. A query is simply a more formal way to sort and filter.

 Filters and Queries   Temporarily narrow down the number of records that appear, according to criteria you select. Using a filter is easier and quicker than using a query, but you can't save a filter as a separate object for later use. (However, you can save a filter as a query.)

Queries enable you to specify which fields you want to see, the order in which the fields should appear, the filter criteria for each field, and the order in which you want each field sorted.

CREATING A SIMPLE QUERY USING QUERY WIZARD

The easiest way to create a query is with a Query Wizard, and the easiest Query Wizard is the Simple Query Wizard.

The Simple Query Wizard enables you to select the fields you want to display—and that's all. You don't get to set criteria for including individual records, and you don't get to specify a sort order. This kind of simple query is useful when you want to weed out extraneous fields, but you still want to see every record.

 Select Query The query that the Simple Query Wizard creates is a very basic version of a Select query. The Select query is the most common query type. With a Select query, you can select records, sort them, filter them, and perform simple calculations (such as counting and averaging) on the results.

To create a simple Select query with the Simple Query Wizard, follow these steps:

1. Open the database you want to work with and click the Queries tab.

2. Click the New button. The New Query dialog box appears.

3. Click Simple Query Wizard and click OK. The first box of the Simple Query Wizard appears (see Figure 12.1).

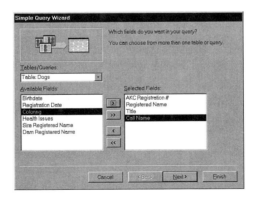

FIGURE 12.1 The Simple Query Wizard first asks which fields you want to include.

4. In the Tables/Queries drop-down list, choose the table from which you want to select fields.

5. Click a field name in the Available Fields list and click the > button to move it to the Selected Fields list. Do the same for any other fields you want to move, or move them all at once with the >> button.

6. Select another table or query from the Tables/Queries list and add some of its fields to the Selected Fields list if you want. When you finish adding fields, click Next.

7. You're asked whether you want a Detail or a Summary query. Choose whichever you want; if you're not sure, stick with Detail, the default. If you choose Summary, the Summary Options button becomes available, which you can click to open a dialog box of summary options. When you're finished, click Next. The next dialog box appears (see Figure 12.2).

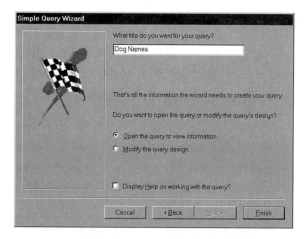

FIGURE 12.2   Enter a title for your query.

8. Enter a title for the query in the What Title Do You Want For Your Query? text box.

9. Click Finish to view the query results. Figure 12.3 shows my results.

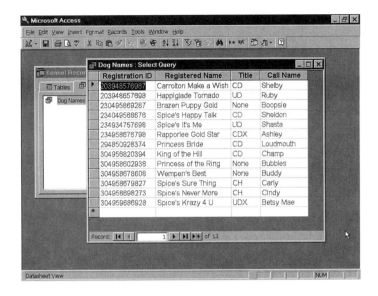

FIGURE 12.3 The results of my Select query.

This simple query is actually too simple; it has limited usefulness and doesn't show off any of Access's powerful query features. You could get the same results by hiding certain columns in Datasheet view. Luckily, the Select query is much more powerful than the Simple Query Wizard makes it appear, as you see in the next lesson. But before you go there, take a look at a few basics that apply to any query.

WORKING WITH QUERY RESULTS

The query results appear in Datasheet view, as shown in Figure 12.3. You can do anything to the records that you can do in a normal Datasheet view, including copy and delete records and change field entries.

For example, you may want to update a sales database to change the Last Contacted field (a date) to today for every record. From your query results window, you could make that change. Or perhaps you want to delete all records for customers who haven't made a purchase in the last two years. You could delete the records from the query results window, and they would disappear from the table too.

Of course, with the latter example, it would be easier if the records were sorted according to the field in question—and the Simple Query Wizard you learned about in this lesson won't enable you to sort. However, there are more powerful Query Wizards that enable you to choose more options.

SAVING A QUERY

When you create a query, Access saves it automatically. You don't need to do anything special to save it. Just close the query window and look on the Queries tab of the Database window. You see the query on the list.

RERUNNING A QUERY

At any time, you can re-run your query. If the data has changed since the last time you ran the query, those changes will be represented. To re-run a query, follow these steps:

1. Open the database containing the query.

2. Click the Queries tab in the Database window.

3. Double-click the query you want to re-run, or click it once and click the Open button (see Figure 12.4).

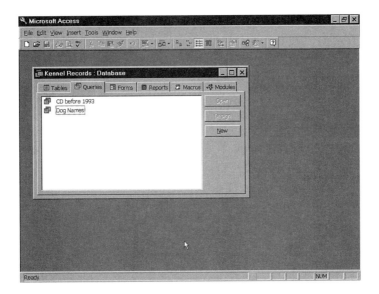

FIGURE 12.4   You can redisplay any query by opening it from the Queries tab.

PRINTING QUERY RESULTS

The query results window not only edits like a datasheet, but the window also prints like one. To print the query results, do the following:

1. Make sure the query results window is active.

2. Select File, Print or press Ctrl+P. The Print dialog box appears.

3. Select whatever print options you want, and then click OK.

If you don't want to set any print options, you can simply click the Print button on the toolbar to print, bypassing the Print dialog box.

OPENING A QUERY IN QUERY DESIGN VIEW

Query Design view is much like Table Design view and Form Design view, both of which you encountered earlier in this part. In Query Design view, you can change the rules that govern your query results.

To open an existing query in Query Design view, follow these steps:

1. Open the database that contains the query you want to edit. Click the Queries tab.

2. Click the query you want to edit, and then click the Design button.

Figure 12.5 shows our simple query as it looks in Query Design view. (This query has only one table. If it had more than one, each table would be displayed in a separate box listing its fields.)

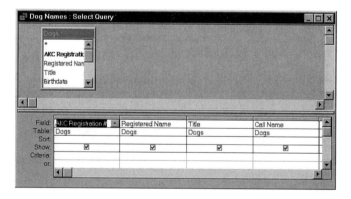

FIGURE 12.5 In Query Design view, you can edit a query you have created.

STARTING A NEW QUERY IN QUERY DESIGN VIEW

Instead of using the Simple Query Wizard to begin your query, you can begin a query from scratch in Query Design view. As you become more familiar with Access queries, you might find that this is faster and easier than using a wizard.

To begin a new query in Query Design view, follow these steps:

1. Open the database in which you want the query.

2. Click the Queries tab in the Database window.

3. Click the New button.

4. Click Design View and click OK. The Show Table dialog box appears, listing all the tables in the database.

5. Select the table you want to work with and click the Add button.

6. Repeat step 5 for each table you want to add.

 Table Relationships   Don't forget that if you use more than one table, a relationship must already be established between the tables. See the section, "Understanding Relationships" in Lesson 11, for more information on relationships.

7. Click Close after you finish adding tables. The Query Design view window opens, as in Figure 12.1, but no fields are selected yet.

ADDING FIELDS TO A QUERY

If you created your query from scratch (as in the preceding set of steps), the first task you need to do is add the fields with which you want to work. You can also use this same procedure to add additional fields to an existing query.

There are three ways to add a field to a query; the easiest method is to double-click the field name in the field list. It moves to the first available slot in the query grid.

DELETING FIELDS

There are two ways to delete a field from your query:

- Click anywhere in the column and select Edit, Delete Column.

- Position the mouse pointer directly above the column so the pointer turns into a down-pointing black arrow. Click to select the entire column, and then press the Delete key or click the Cut button on the toolbar.

If you cut the column instead of deleting it, you can paste it back into the query. Just select the column where you want it, and then click the Paste button or choose Edit, Paste. Be careful, however, because the pasted column will replace the selected one; the selected column doesn't move over to make room for it. Select an empty column if you don't want to replace an existing one.

ADDING CRITERIA

You use criteria to choose which records will appear in your query results.

To set criteria for a field that you have added to your query, follow these steps:

1. In Query Design view, click the Criteria row in the desired field's column.

2. Type the criteria you want to use, as shown in Figure 12.6. Table 12.1 provides some examples you could have entered in Figure 12.6, as well as the subsequent results.

In Figure 12.6, Access added # symbols because you are working with a date. For other types of criteria, Access adds other symbols, such as quotation marks around a text or number string.

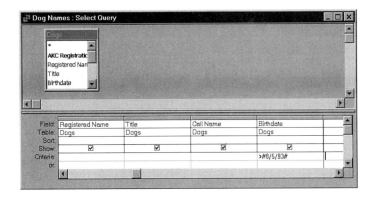

FIGURE 12.6 Enter criteria into the Criteria row in the appropriate field's column.

TABLE 12.1   SAMPLE CRITERIA FOR QUERIES

ENTER THIS...	TO GET RECORDS WHERE THIS VALUE IS...
8/5/93	Exactly 8/5/93
<8/5/93	Before 8/5/93
>8/5/93	After 8/5/93
>=8/5/93	On or after 8/5/93
<=8/5/93	On or before 8/5/93
Not <8/5/93	Not before 8/5/93
Not >8/5/93	Not after 8/5/93

 Text, Too   You can also enter text as a criterion. The < and > (before and after) operators apply to alphabetical order with text. For instance, <C finds text that begins with A or B.

Did you notice the "or" row under the Criteria row in Figure 12.6? You can enter more criteria using that line. The query will find records where any of the criteria is true. When you enter criteria into the "or" row, another "or" row appears, so you can enter more.

When you have two criteria that must both be true, you can put them both together in a single Criteria row with the word "and." For instance, you might want birth dates that were between 12/1/93 and 12/1/95. You could put all that in a single Criteria row, like this: >12/1/93 and <12/1/95.

SORTING A FIELD IN A QUERY

After all this complicated criteria discussion, you will be happy to know that sorting is fairly straightforward. To sort any field, just follow these steps from the query results window:

1. Click in the Sort Row for the field you want to sort. A drop-down arrow appears.

2. Open the drop-down list and select Ascending or Descending.

Later, if you want to cancel sorting for this field, repeat these steps, but select not sorted.

In this lesson, you learned how a query can help you find the information you need, how to create a simple query using the Simple Query Wizard, and how to modify and strengthen your queries.

Working with Presentations

13

In this lesson, you learn how to display a presentation in different views, and how to give your presentation a professional and consistent look.

Changing Views

PowerPoint can display your presentation in different views. Having the option of selecting a view makes it easier to perform certain tasks. Figure 13.1 shows the available views.

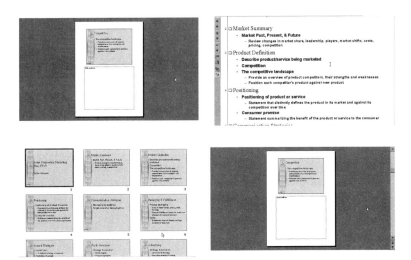

Figure 13.1   You can change views to make a task easier.

To change views, open the View menu and choose the desired view:

- Slide view   You can add both text and art on a slide-by-slide basis.

- Outline view   Shows the overall organization of the presentation.

- Slide Sorter view   Enables you to rearrange the slides.

- Notes Pages view   You can type speaker notes

A quicker way to switch views is to click the button for the desired view at the bottom of the presentation window, as shown in Figure 13.2.

FIGURE 13.2   Use these buttons to change views.

MOVING FROM SLIDE TO SLIDE

When you have more than one slide in your presentation, you will need to move from one slide to the next to work with a specific slide. The procedure for selecting a slide depends on the view you are currently using:

- In Outline view, use the scroll bar to display the slide with which you want to work. Click the Slide icon (the icon to the left of the slide's title) to select the slide, or click anywhere inside the text to edit it.

- In Slide view or Notes Pages view, click the Previous Slide or Next Slide button just below the vertical scroll bar (as shown in Figure 13.3), or drag the box inside the scroll bar until the desired slide number is displayed, or press Page Up or Page Down.

- In Slide Sorter view, click the desired slide. A thick border appears around the selected slide.

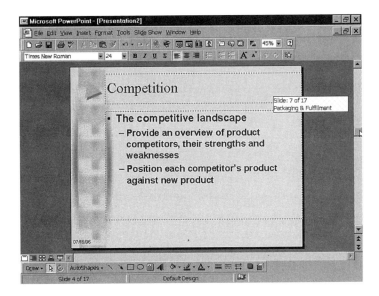

FIGURE 13.3   Use the Previous Slide and Next Slide buttons to move between slides in Slide view or Notes Pages view.

SLIDE MINIATURE WINDOW

The Slide Miniature window is a new feature in PowerPoint 97 (see Figure 13.4). When the feature is active, it displays the currently selected slide in a small window on top of whatever view you're using. To turn Slide Miniature on or off, select View, Slide Miniature. You can also close the Slide Miniature window by clicking its Close button. To move the window around onscreen, drag its title bar to a new location.

In Outline view, the Slide Miniature shows a color version of the selected slide. In all other views, it shows an alternate version of the slide. For example, if you are currently displaying the slides onscreen in color, the Slide Miniature window shows them in black-and-white. Conversely, if the slides are displayed in black-and-white, the Slide Miniature window shows them in color.

The Slide Miniature window is especially useful if you are developing a presentation for two different medias—for example, an on-screen presentation and a black-and-white set of printouts. Slide Miniature helps you keep an eye on the look of the slides so you do not inadvertently make a change to a color slide, for example, that would make it look unattractive or illegible when printed in black-and-white.

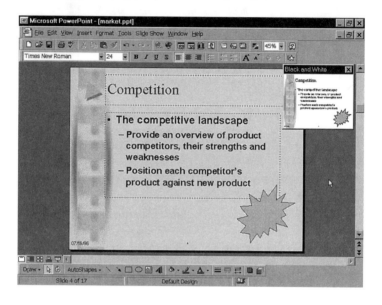

FIGURE 13.4 The Slide Miniature provides a thumbnail sketch of the current slide.

EDITING TEXT IN OUTLINE VIEW

Outline view provides the easiest way to edit text (see Figure 13.5). Click to move the insertion point where you want it and then type your text. Press the Delete key to delete characters to the right of the insertion point, or press the Backspace key to delete characters to the left.

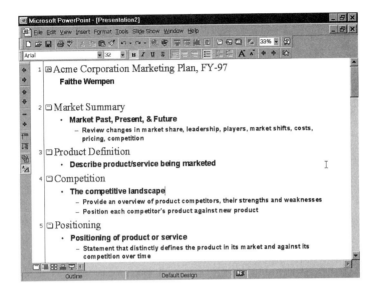

FIGURE 13.5   Switch to Outline view to edit text.

To select text, hold down the left mouse button and drag the mouse over the desired text. You can then press Delete or Backspace to delete the text, or you can drag the text where you want to move it.

CHANGING THE TEXT'S OUTLINE LEVEL

As you can see from Figure 13.5, your presentation is organized in a multilevel outline format. The slides are at the top level of the outline, and each slide's contents are subordinate under that slide. Some slides have multiple levels of subordination (for example, a bulleted list within a bulleted list).

You can easily change an object's level in Outline view with the Tab key:

- Click the text, and then press the Tab key or click the Demote button on the Outlining toolbar to demote it one level in the outline.

- Click the text, and then press Shift+Tab or click the Promote button on the Outlining toolbar to promote it one level in the outline.

In most cases, subordinate items on a slide appear as items in a bulleted list.

MOVING A LINE IN OUTLINE VIEW

As you work in Outline view, you may find that some paragraphs need to be rearranged. One easy way to rearrange text is with the Move Up and Move Down buttons on the Outlining toolbar.

To move a paragraph up in the outline, select it and click the Move Up button; to move a paragraph down in the outline, select it and click the Move Down button.

Dragging Paragraphs You can quickly change the position or level of a paragraph by dragging it up, down, left, or right. To drag a paragraph, move the mouse pointer to the left side of the paragraph until the pointer turns into a four-headed arrow. Then hold down the left mouse button and drag the paragraph to the desired position.

EDITING IN SLIDE VIEW

Slide view provides an easy way to edit all objects on a slide, including text and graphics. As shown in Figure 13.6, you can edit an object by clicking or double-clicking it. For text, click the object to select it, and then click where you want the insertion point moved. For graphics, double-click the object to bring up a set of tools that will help you edit it.

The following sections and Lesson 14, "Enhancing and Giving Presentations" discuss placing graphics on slides, and manipulating graphics.

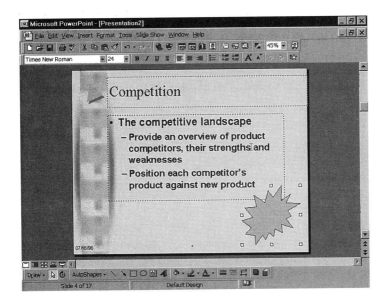

FIGURE 13.6   Slide view enables you to edit both text and graphics.

GIVING YOUR SLIDES A PROFESSIONAL LOOK

PowerPoint comes with dozens of professionally designed slides you can use as templates for your own presentations. That is, you can apply one of these predesigned slides to an already existing presentation to give the slides in your presentation a consistent look.

Template   A template is a predesigned slide that comes with PowerPoint. When you select a template, PowerPoint applies the color scheme and general layout of the slide to each slide in your presentation.

You can also make global changes to the entire presentation in another way—you can alter the Slide Master. The Slide Master is not really a slide, but it looks like one. It's a design grid on which you make changes, and these changes affect every slide in the presentation. For example, if you want a graphic to appear on every slide, you can place it on the Slide Master instead of pasting it onto each slide individually. When you apply a template, you are actually applying that template to the Slide Master, which in turn applies the template's formatting to each slide.

APPLYING A PRESENTATION DESIGN TEMPLATE

You can apply a different template to your presentation at any time, no matter how you originally create your presentation. To change the template, follow these steps:

1. Click the Apply Design button on the Standard toolbar, or choose Format, Apply Design. The Apply Design dialog box appears (see Figure 13.7).

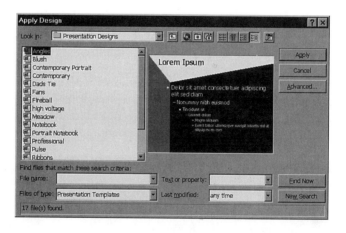

FIGURE 13.7   Choose a different template from the Apply Design dialog box.

2. Click a template name in the list. A sample of the template appears to the right of the list.

3. When you find a template you want to use, click Apply.

USING AUTOLAYOUTS

Whereas templates enable you to change the color and design of a presentation, AutoLayouts enable you to set the structure of a single slide in a presentation. For example, if you want a graph and a picture on a slide, you can choose an AutoLayout that positions the two items for you.

To use an AutoLayout, do the following:

1. In Slide view, display the slide you want to change.

2. Choose Format, Slide Layout or click the Slide Layout button on the Standard toolbar. The Slide Layout dialog box appears (see Figure 13.8).

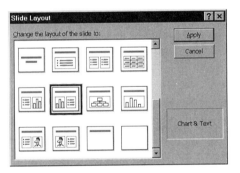

FIGURE 13.8   You can change an individual slide's layout with this dialog box.

3. Click the desired layout, or use the arrow keys to move the selection border to it.

4. Click the Apply button, and PowerPoint applies the selected layout to the current slide.

EDITING THE SLIDE MASTER

Every presentation has a Slide Master that controls the overall appearance and layout of each slide. The Slide Master contains all the formatting information that the template brings to the presentation, such as colors and background patterns, and it also marks where the elements you use from the AutoLayout feature will appear on the slide.

To make changes to the Slide Master for your presentation, follow these steps:

1. Select View, Master, Slide Master. Your Slide Master appears, as in Figure 13.9.

2. Make any changes to the Slide Master, as you'll learn in upcoming lessons in this book. (Anything you can do to a regular slide, you can also do to a Slide Master.)

3. When you're done working with the Slide Master, click the Close button (see Figure 13.9) to return to Normal view.

The two most important elements on the Slide Master are the Title Area and Object Area for the AutoLayout objects. The Title Area contains the formatting specifications for each slide's title; that is, it tells PowerPoint the type size, style, and color to use for the text in the title of each slide. The Object Area contains the formatting specifications for all remaining text on the slide.

For most of PowerPoint's templates, the Object Area sets up specifications for a bulleted list, including the type of bullet, as well as the type styles, sizes, and indents for each item in the list.

In addition to the Title and Object Areas, the Slide Master can contain information about background colors, borders, page numbers, company logos, clip art objects, and any other elements you want to appear on every slide in the presentation.

The Slide Master is like any slide. In the following lesson, when you learn how to add text, graphics, borders, and other objects to a slide, keep in mind that you can add these objects on individual slides or on the Slide Master. When you add the objects to the Slide Master, they appear on every slide in the presentation.

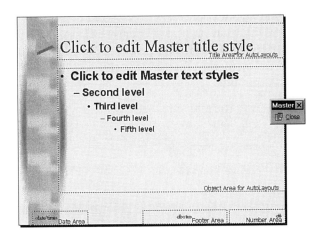

FIGURE 13.9   The Slide Master ensures that all slides in a presentation have a consistent look.

REARRANGING SLIDES IN SLIDE SORTER VIEW

Slide Sorter view shows miniature versions of the slides in your presentation. This enables you to view many of your slides at one time. To rearrange slides in Slide Sorter view, perform the following steps:

1. Switch to Slide Sorter view by selecting View, Slide Sorter or by clicking the Slide Sorter button on the status bar.

2. Move the mouse pointer over the slide you want to move.

3. Press and hold the left mouse button, and drag to the location in which you want to insert the slide. As you drag, a line appears (as shown in Figure 13.10), showing where you are moving the slide.

Destination Not in View?   If you have more than six slides in your presentation, you may not be able to see the slide's destination onscreen. Don't worry. Just drag the slide in the direction of the destination, and the display will scroll in that direction.

 Copying a Slide   You can copy a slide in Slide Sorter view as easily as you can move a slide. Simply hold down the Ctrl key when you drag the slide.

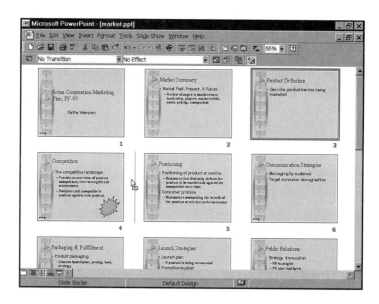

Figure 13.10   Switch to Slide Sorter view.

4. When the vertical line is in the location where you want the slide, release the mouse button. PowerPoint places the slide in its new position and shifts the surrounding slides to make room for the new slide.

REARRANGING SLIDES IN OUTLINE VIEW

In Outline view, you see the titles and text that appear on each slide. This view gives you a clearer picture of the content and organization of your presentation than the other views, so you may prefer to rearrange your slides in Outline view. The following steps show you how to do it:

1. Switch to Outline view by choosing View, Outline or by clicking the Outline button.

2. Click the slide number or the slide icon to the left of the slide you want to move. PowerPoint highlights the contents of the entire slide.

 Moving the Contents of a Slide If you just want to insert some of the information from a slide into your presentation, you don't have to move the entire slide. You can move only the slide's data—text and graphics—from one slide to another by selecting only what you want to move and dragging it to its new location.

3. Move the mouse pointer over the selected slide icon, press and hold the mouse button, and drag the slide up or down in the outline. Or, select the slide and click the Move Up or Move Down button on the Outlining toolbar (see Figure 13.11).

4. When the slide is at the desired new position, release the mouse button. (Be careful not to drop the slide in the middle of another slide. If you do, choose Edit, Undo and try again.)

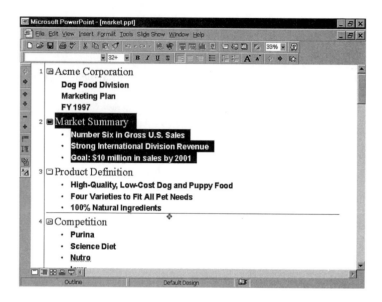

FIGURE 13.11   Drag the selected icon, or click the Move Up or Move Down button.

Collapsing the Outline   You can collapse the outline to show only the slide titles. This enables you to view more slides at one time and rearrange the slides more easily. To collapse the outline, click the Collapse All button on the Outlining toolbar (refer to Figure 13.11). To restore the outline, click the Expand All button.

In this lesson, you learned how to display a presentation in different views, give your presentation a professional and consistent look.

ENHANCING AND GIVING PRESENTATIONS

*In this lesson, you learn how to
enhance your presentation with additional elements.*

ADDING ELEMENTS TO SLIDES

There are many elements that you can add to a presentation to
make information more enjoyable to view. Some of these elements are text boxes, columns and lists, pictures, sounds, and
video clips, charts, and even URL hyperlinks.

Keep in mind that you can add the same types of things you
would add to a document or spreadsheet, to a presentation; we
are only going to cover a few.

ADDING A TEXT BOX

As you have learned in the previous lesson, you can put text on a
slide by typing text in Outline view or by filling in the blanks on
an AutoLayout. However, both these methods provide fairly generic results. If you want to type additional text on a slide, you
must first create a text box.

To create a text box, perform the following steps:

1. Switch to Slide view or Slide Sorter view. Slide view may
   give you a clearer view of your work area.

2. If you want the text box to appear on a new slide, insert a
   slide into the presentation.

3. Click the Text Box button on the Drawing toolbar.

4. Position the mouse pointer where you want the upper-left corner of the box to appear.

5. Press and hold the left mouse button and drag to the right until the box is the desired width. Release the mouse button, and a one-line text box appears (see Figure 14.1).

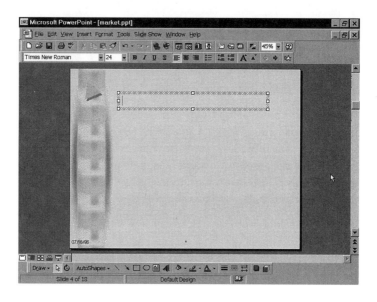

Figure 14.1 You can enter text in the text box.

6. Type the text that you want to appear in the text box. When you reach the right side of the box, PowerPoint wraps the text to the next line and makes the box one line deeper. To start a new paragraph, press Enter.

7. When you are done, click anywhere outside the text box to see how the text will appear on the finished slide.

Adding a Bulleted List

When you enter new slides in Outline view, the default layout is a simple bulleted list. However, you can also create a bulleted list yourself in a text box that you add to a slide, without relying on an AutoLayout. Follow these steps to change some regular text in a text box to a bulleted list:

1. Click inside the paragraph you want to transform into a bulleted list, or select one or more paragraphs.

2. Select Format, Bullet. The Bullet dialog box appears.

3. Select the Use A Bullet check box to enable bullet use and click OK.

4. PowerPoint transforms the selected text into a bulleted list. (If you press Enter at the end of a bulleted paragraph, the next paragraph starts with a bullet.)

 Moving a Bulleted Item   You can move an item in a bulleted list by clicking the item's bullet and then dragging the bullet up or down in the list.

Adding a WordArt Object

PowerPoint comes with an auxiliary program called WordArt that can help you create graphics text effects. To insert a WordArt object into a slide, perform the following steps:

1. In Slide view, display the slide on which you want to place the WordArt object.

2. Click the WordArt button on the Drawing toolbar (at the bottom of the screen). The WordArt Gallery dialog box appears, showing many samples of WordArt types.

3. Click the sample that best represents the WordArt type you want, and then click OK. The Edit WordArt Text dialog box appears (see Figure 14.2).

4. Choose a font and font size from the respective drop-down lists.

5. Type the text you want to use in the Text box.

6. Click OK, and PowerPoint creates the WordArt text on your slide, as shown in Figure 14.2.

FIGURE 14.2   Finished WordArt on a slide, with the WordArt toolbar below it.

To edit the WordArt object, double-click it to display the WordArt toolbar and text entry box. Enter your changes, and then click outside the WordArt object. You can move the object by dragging its border, or you can resize it by dragging a handle.

ADDING ACTION BUTTONS

One way to advance or go back in a slide show is to press the Page Down key or Page Up key on the keyboard. This simple method works fine, except for two things:

• In a kiosk-type setting, you may not want the audience to have access to the computer's keyboard.

- This method simply plods from slide to slide, with no opportunity to jump to special slides or quickly jump to the beginning or end.

There is a new feature that solves this problem—PowerPoint 97 allows you to add *action buttons* to slides. Action buttons are like controls on an audio CD player: They let you jump to any slide quickly, go backward, go forward, or even stop the presentation.

 Same Controls on All Slides? If you want to add the same action buttons to all slides in the presentation, add the action buttons to the Slide Master. To display the Slide Master, select View, Master, Slide Master.

To add an action button to a slide, follow these steps:

1. Display the slide in Slide view.

2. Select Slide Show, Action Buttons, and then pick a button from the palette that appears next to the command (see Figure 14.3). For instance, if you want to create a button that advances to the next slide, you might choose the button with the arrow pointing to the right.

FIGURE 14.3 Choose the button you think your reader will most strongly identify with the action you're going to assign to it.

3. Your mouse pointer turns into a crosshair. Drag to draw a box on the slide where you want the button to appear.

4. Choose the type of action you want to happen when the user clicks the button. Most of the time you will choose Hyperlink To. Your complete list of choices includes the following:

- None

- Hyperlink To This can be a slide, an Internet hyperlink, a document on your computer—just about anything.

- Run Program You can choose to have a program start when the user clicks the button.

- Run Macro If you have recorded a macro, you can have the user run it from this button.

- Object Action If you have embedded (OLE) objects in the presentation, you can have PowerPoint activate one when this button is clicked.

5. Open the drop-down list for the type of action you chose and select the exact action (such as Next Slide). Or, if you chose Run Program, click the Browse button and locate the program you want to run.

6. (Optional) If you want a sound to play when the user clicks the button, select the Play Sound check box and choose a sound from its drop-down list.

7. (Optional) If you want the button to look animated when the user clicks it (a nice little extra), leave the Animate Click check box marked.

8. Click OK, and your button appears on the slide.

9. View the presentation to try out the button.

Figure 14.4 shows three buttons added to a slide. Actually, they were added to the Slide Master, so the same buttons appear on each slide in the presentation. This kind of consistency gives the reader a feeling of comfort and control.

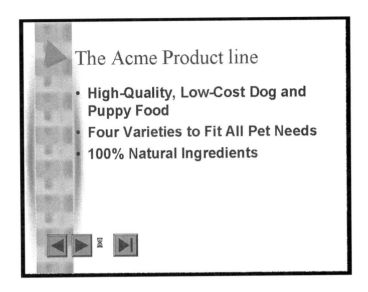

FIGURE 14.4   These control buttons display various slides in the presentation.

    Don't Group   Each action button must be an independent object on the slide. If you group them together, they won't work properly.

ADDING URL HYPERLINKS

You added action buttons to a slide in the previous section, that moved the presentation from slide to slide. Well, you can also assign links to Web addresses (URLs) to a button. For instance, you might have a button that takes you to your company's home page (the top page in your company's Internet site) at the bottom of every slide.

Say you've started a new presentation based on a design template for online use. It already has buttons for Previous and Next. You want to set the Home button to jump to your Web site's home page when clicked (http://www.mysite.com). Perform the following steps:

1. Choose View, Master, Slide Master. (The navigation buttons are on the Slide Master.)

2. Click the Home button so that selection handles appear around it.

3. Choose Slide Show, Action Settings. The Action Settings dialog box appears.

4. Click the Hyperlink To button.

5. Open the Hyperlink To drop-down list and select URL.

6. In the dialog box that appears, type the URL you want to link to.

7. Click OK twice to close both dialog boxes.

 Start the Show!   Clicking the Slide Show button is the fastest way to start a slide show. However, you can also start a slide show by selecting View, Slide Show or by selecting Slide Show, View Show.

Now it's time to test your hyperlink. View the slide in Slide Show view, and click the button with your mouse. Your Web browser should start and the selected URL should load in it, provided your Internet connection is active.

Viewing an Onscreen Slide Show

You can preview a slide show at any time to see how the show looks in real life. To view a slide show, perform the following steps:

1. Open the presentation you want to view.

2. Click the Slide Show button at the bottom of the presentation window. The first slide in the presentation appears full-screen.

3. To display the next or previous slide, do one of the following:

- To display the next slide, click the left mouse button, or press the Page Down key, or press the right arrow or down arrow key.

- To display the previous slide, click the right mouse button, or press the Page Up key, or press the left arrow or up arrow key.

- To quit the slide show, press the Esc key.

CONTROLLING THE SLIDE SHOW

While you view a slide show, you can do more than just move from slide to slide. When you move your mouse, notice the triangle in a box at the bottom left corner of the slide show (see Figure 14.5). Click that button, and PowerPoint displays a pop-up menu that contains commands you can use as you actually give the presentation. Those commands are outlined in the following list:

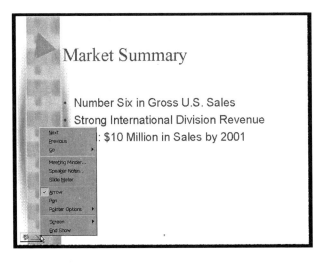

FIGURE 14.5 You can control the slide show while you present it with this menu.

- The Next and Previous commands enable you to move from slide to slide. (It's easier to change slides if you use other methods, though.)

- Choose Go, Slide Navigator to bring up a dialog box listing every slide in the presentation. You can jump quickly to any slide with it. You can also jump to a slide with a specific title (if you know it) by selecting Go, Title and choosing the title from the list.

- Click Meeting Minder to bring up a window where you can take notes as the meeting associated with your presentation progresses.

- Choose Speaker Notes to view your notes for the slide.

- Choose Slide Meter to open a dialog box that enables you to control the timing between slides.

- Arrow and Pen are mouse options; Arrow is the default. Your mouse can serve as an arrow to point out parts of the slide, or it can serve as a pen to write comments on the slide or circle key areas as you give your presentation. Keep in mind, however, that it is very difficult to write legibly if you use an ordinary mouse or trackball.

- Pointer Options enables you to choose a color for the pen and indicate whether to display or hide the pointer.

- Screen opens a submenu that enables you to pause the show, blank the screen, and erase any pen marks you made on the slide.

- End Show takes you back to PowerPoint's slide editing window.

SETTING SLIDE SHOW OPTIONS

Depending on the type of show you're presenting, you may find it useful to make some fine adjustments to the way the show runs, such as making it run in a window (the default is full-screen) or showing only certain slides. You'll find these controls and more in the Set Up Show dialog box (shown in Figure 14.6). To open it, choose Slide Show, Set Up Show.

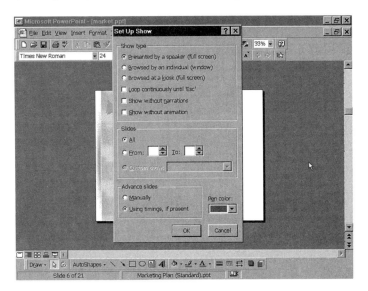

FIGURE 14.6   Use the Set Up Show dialog box to give Power-Point instructions about how to present your slide show.

In the Set Up Show dialog box, you can do the following:

- Choose in which medium the presentation is going to be shown. Your choices are Presented by a Speaker (Full Screen), Browsed by an Individual (Window), and Browsed at a Kiosk (Full Screen).

- Choose whether to loop the slide show continuously or just show it once. You might want to loop it continuously if it were running unaided at a kiosk at a trade show, for instance.

- Show without narration, if you have created any.

- Show without animation, if you have added any.

- Show all the slides or a range of them (which you enter in the From and To boxes).

- Choose a custom show if you have created one. (To create a custom show, such as one that contains a subset of the main show's slides, select Slide Show, Custom Show.)

- Choose whether to advance slides manually or by using timings you set up.

- Choose a pen color.

PRINTING PRESENTATIONS, NOTES, AND HANDOUTS

The quickest way to print is to use all the default settings. You don't get to make any decisions about your output, but you do get your printout without delay. To print a quick copy, choose File, Print, and click OK.

When you use either of these methods for printing, you get a printout of your entire presentation in whatever view is on-screen. The following list describes the type of printout you can expect from each view:

- Slide view   The entire presentation prints in Landscape orientation with one slide per page. Each slide fills an entire page.

- Outline view   The entire outline prints in Portrait orientation.

- Slide Sorter view   The entire presentation prints in Portrait orientation with six slides per page.

- Notes Pages view   The entire presentation prints in Portrait orientation with one slide per page. Each slide prints with its notes beneath it.

In this lesson, you learned how to enhance your presentation with additional elements.

USING AND MANAGING MAIL

LESSON

15

*In this lesson, you learn to read, save,
answer, and close a message. You also learn to delete and undelete
messages, forward messages, compose messages, check your spelling,
attach files, and send mail.*

READING MAIL

Each time you open Outlook, your Inbox folder appears (by default), and any new messages you've received are waiting for you (see Figure 15.1). As you can see in this figure, the Inbox provides important information about each message. For example, two of the messages have attachments, and some have Low or High priority flags.

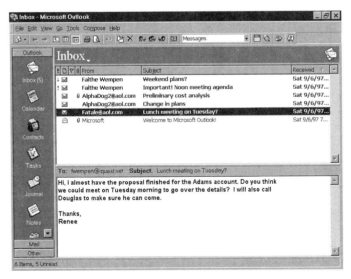

FIGURE 15.1 Review the sender and subject before opening your mail.

To open and read your messages, follow these steps:

1. Double-click a mail message to open it. Figure 15.2 shows an open message.

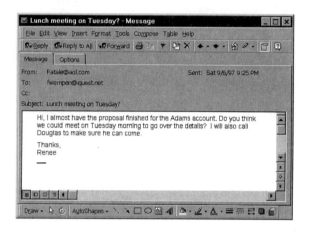

FIGURE 15.2 The Message window displays the message and some tools for handling this message or moving on to another.

2. To read the next or previous mail message in the Inbox, click the Previous Item or the Next Item button on the toolbar. Or you can open the View menu, choose Previous or Next, and choose Item.

 Item Outlook uses the word *item* to describe a mail message, an attached file, an appointment or meeting, a task, or some other Outlook data element. Item is a generic term in Outlook that describes the currently selected element.

You can mark messages as read or unread by choosing Edit, Mark As Read Or Edit, Mark As Unread. Outlook automatically marks messages as read when you open them. You might, however, want to mark messages yourself once in a while (as a reminder, for example). You might want to mark mail messages as read so that you don't read them again, or you might want to mark important mail as unread so that you'll be sure to open it and read it again. Additionally, you can mark all the messages in the Inbox as read at one time by choosing Edit, Mark All As Read.

SAVING MAIL TO A FOLDER

Although you'll delete some mail after you read and respond to it, you'll want to save other messages for future reference. You can save a message to any folder you want, but you should use a logical filing system to ensure that you'll be able to find each message again later. Outlook offers several methods for organizing your mail.

The easiest method of saving mail to a folder is to move it to one of Outlook's built-in mail folders. You can use any of the folders to store your mail, or you can create new folders. To move messages to an existing folder, follow these steps:

1. Select one message (by clicking it) or select multiple messages (by Ctrl+clicking).

2. Choose Edit, Move To Folder or click the Move To Folder tool button on the toolbar. The Move Items dialog box appears (see Figure 15.3).

3. Select the folder you want to move the item to and click OK. Outlook moves the item to the folder for you.

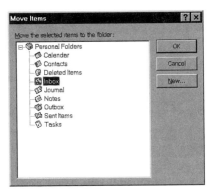

FIGURE 15.3   Choose the folder to which you want to move the selected message(s).

To view the message(s) you've moved, choose the folder from the Outlook Bar or the Folder List. Then click the item you want to view.

SAVING AN ATTACHMENT

You will often receive messages that have one or more files or other items attached. A paper clip icon beside the message represents an attachment. You'll want to save any attachments sent to you so that you can open, modify, print, or otherwise use the document.

To save an attachment, follow these steps:

1. Open the message containing an attachment by double-clicking the message. The attachment appears as an icon in the message text (see Figure 15.4).

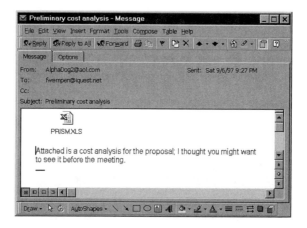

FIGURE 15.4   An icon represents the attached file.

2. (Optional) You can open the attachment from within the message by double-clicking the icon. The application in which the document was created (Word or Excel, for example) opens and displays the document in the window, ready for you to read. Close the application by choosing File, Exit.

3. In the message, select the attachment you want to save and choose File, Save Attachments. The Save Attachment dialog box appears (see Figure 15.5).

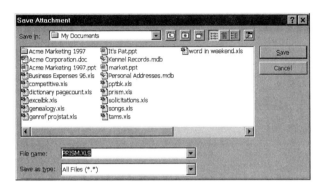

FIGURE 15.5   Save the attachment to a convenient folder.

4. Choose the folder in which you want to save the attachment and click Save. (You can change the name of the file if you want.) The dialog box closes, and you're returned to the Message window. You can open the attachment at any time from the application in which it was created.

 Save Attachment Versus Save As   You also can save the attachment by choosing File, Save Attachment. However, do not confuse this command with File, Save As. The latter command saves the e-mail message itself, rather than the attachment.

ANSWERING MAIL

You may want to reply to a message after you read it. The Message window enables you to answer a message immediately, or at a later time if you prefer. To reply to any given message, open the message and follow these steps:

1. Click the Reply button or choose Compose, Reply. The
    Reply Message window appears, with the original message
    in the message text area and the sender of the message
    already filled in for you (see Figure 15.6).

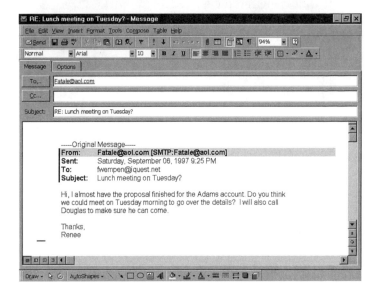

FIGURE 15.6   Reply to a message quickly and easily.

Reply to All   If you receive a message that has also
been sent to others besides yourself—as either a message or a carbon copy (cc)—you can click the Reply To
All button (instead of the Reply button) to send your reply
to each person who received the original message.

2. The insertion point is in the message text area, ready for
    you to enter your reply. Enter the text.

3. When you finish your reply, click the Send button or
    choose File, Send. Outlook sends the message.

When you reply to a message, by default the reply quotes the original message. Each line has a > sign in front of it, to distinguish it from new text you add. You can type your reply at the top of the message, above the quoted text, or you can intersperse your reply lines between the quoted lines so that you are replying to specific statements. You can even delete some of the original message so you are only quoting the lines to which you want to reply.

FORWARDING MAIL

Suppose you want to forward e-mail that you receive from a co-worker to another person who has an interest in the message. You can forward any message that you receive, and you can even add comments to the message if you want. (Forwarding is different than replying because you are sending an e-mail to someone who wasn't originally a recipient.)

You forward an open message or a selected message from the Inbox message list in the same way. To forward mail, follow these steps:

1. Select or open the message you want to forward. Then click the Forward button or choose Compose, Forward. The FW Message dialog box appears (see Figure 15.7).

2. In the To text box, enter the names of the people to whom you want to forward the mail. (If you want to choose a person's name from a list, click the To button to display the Select Names dialog box, and then select the person's name. If you enter multiple names in the To box, separate the names with a semicolon and a space.

3. (Optional) In the Cc text box, enter the names of anyone to whom you want to forward copies of the message (or click the Cc button and choose the name from the list that appears).

4. In the message area of the window, enter any message you want to send with the forwarded text. The text you type will be a different color.

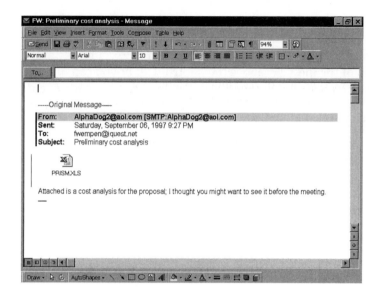

FIGURE 15.7 When you forward a message, the original message appears at the bottom of the message window.

5. Click the Send button or choose File, Send.

PRINTING MAIL

You can print e-mail messages, whether they're open or not. To print an unopened message, select the message in the message list of the Inbox or other folder and choose File, Print. If the message is already open, you can follow these steps:

1. Open the message in Outlook.

2. Click the Print button on the toolbar to print using defaults.

3. In the Print dialog box, click OK to print one copy of the entire message using the printer's default settings.

Deleting Mail

You may want to store some important messages, but you definitely want to delete much of the mail you receive. After you answer a question or responded to a request, you probably don't have need for a reminder of that transaction. You can easily delete messages in Outlook when you finish with them.

To delete an e-mail message that is open, click the Delete button on the toolbar. If you have modified the message in any way, a confirmation message appears from the Office Assistant or as a message dialog box. Otherwise, the message is moved to the Deleted Items folder without warning.

If you're in the Inbox and you want to delete one or more messages from the message list, select a message to delete. (You can select multiple messages to delete at once by holding down Ctrl and clicking each message or by clicking the first message in a block and then holding down Shift while clicking the last message in the block.) Then click the Delete button on the toolbar.

Undeleting Items

If you change your mind and want to get back items you've deleted, you can usually retrieve them from the Deleted Items folder. By default, when you delete an item, it doesn't disappear from your system; it merely moves to the Deleted Items folder.

To retrieve a deleted item from the Deleted Items folder, follow these steps:

1. Click the Deleted Items icon in the Outlook Bar to open the folder.

2. Select the items you want to retrieve and drag them to the folder containing the same type of items on the Outlook Bar. When retrieving a deleted message from a friend or colleague, for example, you probably would want to drag it back to the Inbox. Alternatively, you can choose Edit, Move To Folder, choose the folder to which you want to move the selected items, and click OK.

EMPTYING THE DELETED ITEMS FOLDER

If you're really sure you want to delete the items in the Deleted Items folder, you can erase them from your system. To delete items in the Deleted Items folder, follow these steps:

1. In the Outlook Bar, choose the Outlook group and select the Deleted Items folder. All deleted items in that folder appear in the message list, as shown in Figure 15.8.

2. To permanently delete an item, select it in the Deleted Items folder, and then click the Delete tool button or choose Edit, Delete. You can choose more than one item to delete by holding down the Shift or Ctrl key and clicking each item.

3. Outlook displays a confirmation dialog box asking whether you're sure you want to permanently delete the message. Choose Yes to delete the selected item.

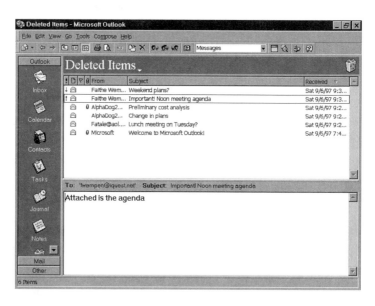

FIGURE 15.8 Deleted messages remain in the Deleted Items folder until you permanently delete them.

Composing a Message

You can send a message to anyone for whom you have an address, regardless of whether he or she is in your address book. In addition to sending a message to one or more recipients, you can send copies of a message to others on your address list. (See Lesson 16, "Managing Contacts," for more information about addressing a message and sending carbon copies.)

To compose a message, follow these steps:

1. In the Outlook Inbox, click the New Mail Message button or choose Compose, New Mail Message. The Untitled—Message window appears (see Figure 15.9).

2. Enter the name of the recipient in the To text box, or click the To button and select the name of the recipient from your Address Book.

3. Enter the name of anyone to whom you want to send a copy of the message in the Cc text box, or click the Cc button and select a name or names from the Address Book.

4. In the Subject text box, enter the subject of the message.

5. Click in the text area, and then enter the text of the message. You do not have to press the Enter key at the end of a line; Outlook automatically wraps the text at the end of a line for you. You can use the Delete and Backspace keys to edit the text you enter. You also may use the Cut, Copy, and Paste functions just as you would when using most application.

6. When you finish typing the message, you can send the message immediately with File, Send or by clicking the Send button.

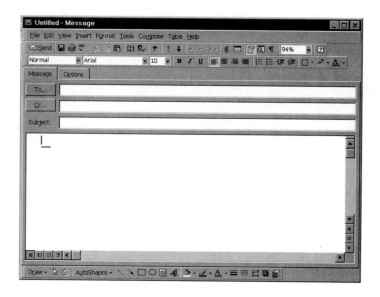

FIGURE 15.9   Compose a new message in the Untitled—
Message window.

If you try to compose a message to someone without entering an
address, Outlook displays the Check Names dialog box, in which
it asks you to create an address. You can search for the name
among the existing addresses, or you can create a new address for
the name in much the same way you would create a new entry in
the Address Book.

FORMATTING TEXT

You can change the format of the text—fonts, bold, italic, and so
on—in your message to make it more attractive, to make it easier
to read, or to add emphasis. Any formatting that you add transfers
with the message to the recipient, if the recipient is using Outlook
as her e-mail client. However, if the recipient is using an e-mail
client other than Outlook, your formatting may not transfer.

By default, if you have Word installed, Outlook asks you the
first time you start it whether you want to use it for message

composition. Figure 15.9 shows e-mail composition with this feature enabled; that's why the tools in Figure 15.9 may seem familiar to Word users. If you don't want to use Word, open the Tools menu and deselect Use Word as E-Mail Editor. Then your message composition screen will display an abbreviated set of formatting tools, rather than Word's complete set.

SPELL CHECKING YOUR E-MAIL

To make a good impression and to maintain your professional image, you should check the spelling in your mail messages before you send them. Outlook includes a spell checker you can use for that purpose. If you're using Word as your e-mail editor, you'll notice that your grammar is automatically checked.

To check the spelling in a message, follow these steps:

1. In the open message, choose Tools, Spelling And Grammar, or click the Spelling And Grammar button on the toolbar (if you are using Word as your editor), or press F7.

2. If the spell checker finds a word whose spelling it questions, it displays the Spelling dialog box (shown in Figure 15.10). From here you can choose from the many options to correct your errors. If it does not find any misspelled words, a dialog box appears with a message that the spelling and grammar check is complete. Click OK to close the dialog box.

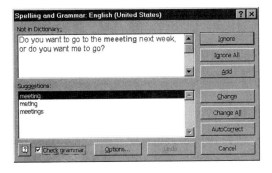

FIGURE 15.10   Check your spelling before sending a message.

3. When the spelling check is complete, Outlook displays a message box telling you that it's done. Click OK to close the dialog box.

ATTACHING A FILE

You can attach any type of file to an Outlook message, which makes for a convenient way of sending your files over the network to your coworkers. You might send Word documents, Excel spreadsheets, PowerPoint presentations, or any other documents you create with your Windows applications.

 Insert Item In addition to attaching files from other programs, you also can attach an Outlook item to a message. An Outlook item can be any document saved in one of your personal folders, including a calendar, contacts, journal, notes, and tasks. You can attach an Outlook item in the same manner you attach a file.

When you send an attached file, it appears as an icon in the message. When the recipient gets the file, he or she can open it within the message or save it for later use. However, the recipient must have the source program that you used to create the file on his or her computer. For instance, if you send a colleague a Microsoft Word file, he must have Microsoft Word to view the file he receives.

To attach a file to a message, follow these steps:

1. In the Message window, position the insertion point in the message text, and then choose Insert, File or click the Insert File toolbar button. The Insert File dialog box appears (see Figure 15.11).

2. From the Look In drop-down list, maneuver to the file you want to attach.

3. Click OK to insert the file into the message. (Figure 15.12 shows an Excel file inserted as an attachment.)

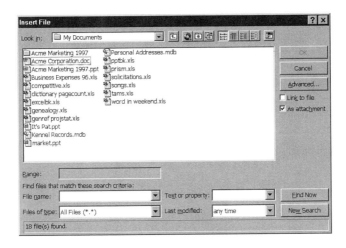

FIGURE 15.11 Select the file you want to attach to a message.

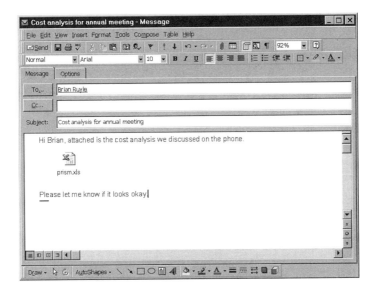

FIGURE 15.12 An inserted attachment.

Insert Objects Just as you can insert an object—a spreadsheet, chart, drawing, presentation, media clip, clip art, and WordArt—in any Windows application that supports Object Linking and Embedding, you also can insert an object into an Outlook e-mail message.

SENDING AND CLOSING MAIL

When you're ready to send your e-mail message, simply click the Send button or choose File, Send.

 AutoSignature Choose Tools, AutoSignature to have Outlook automatically add a message, quotation, or other text at the end of every message you send. Additionally, after you create an autosignature, you can quickly add it to any message by choosing Insert, AutoSignature.

When you finish with a message, you can close it by clicking the Close (X) button in the title bar of the Message window.

In this lesson, you learned to read, save, answer, and close a message. You also learned to delete and undelete messages, forward messages, compose messages, check your spelling, attach files, and send mail.

MANAGING CONTACTS

In this lesson, you learn to use Outlook's Address Book with your e-mail and creating and working with a contacts list.

OPENING THE ADDRESS BOOK

The Address Book stores contact information for the people you need to communicate with so that you don't have to remember e-mail addresses and other contact information.

To open the Postoffice Address List, choose Tools, Address Book or click the Address Book tool button on the toolbar. The Address Book dialog box appears, as shown in Figure 16.1.

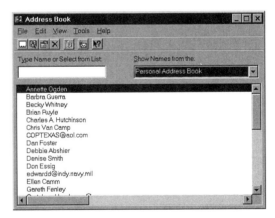

FIGURE 16.1 The Address Book dialog box.

Depending on your setup, you may see Postoffice Address List, Personal Address Book, or Outlook Address List in the Show

Names drop-down list. It all depends on what is available on your PC and what is set as the default. You can easily switch among the available address lists by choosing the one you want from the Show Names drop-down list. The Postoffice Address List is the address list on your company's network; if you are using Outlook on a standalone computer, you will not have this.

USING A POSTOFFICE ADDRESS LIST

If you are using Outlook in a business and your PC is connected to the company network, all the names within your organization usually appear on a Postoffice Address List created by your system's mail administrator. Anytime you want to send or forward an e-mail, you can select the recipients from that list instead of typing in their names manually. If you're using Windows NT on a network, you may or may not have access to the Postoffice Address List, depending on your permissions and rights.

 Postoffice Address List   A list of everyone who has a mailbox in the post office. The Postoffice Address List is controlled by the mail administrator.

USING THE PERSONAL ADDRESS BOOK

Everyone has an Address Book in Outlook, even those who use Outlook at home and are not connected to a network. In the Personal Address Book, you store the names and e-mail addresses of people you contact frequently.

If you do not see a Personal Address Book in the Address Book dialog box, you can easily add it to your resources. Here's how:

1. Close the Address Book dialog box and choose Tools, Services.

2. In the Services tab of the dialog box, click the Add button, choose Personal Address Book from the list, and click OK.

3. In the Personal Address Book dialog box, select your preference (such as where the file is stored) and click OK.

4. Close the Services dialog box and open the Address Book dialog box again; you'll now see the Personal Address Book in the list. You may have to exit and restart Outlook to see it.

COPYING NAMES TO THE PERSONAL ADDRESS BOOK

To add names to the Personal Address Book from the Postoffice Address List (or another address list), follow these steps:

1. Choose Tools, Address Book or click the Address Book tool button on the toolbar. The Address Book dialog box appears (refer to Figure 5.1).

2. Select the list from the Show Names drop-down list that contains the names from which you want to copy (for example, Postoffice Address List).

3. Select the name(s) from the list box, and then click the Add To Personal Address Book button on the toolbar or choose File, Add To Personal Address Book. The name(s) remain on the original list, but Outlook copies them to your Personal Address Book as well.

4. To view your Personal Address Book, Choose Personal Address Book from the Show Names drop-down list. The list changes to display those names you've added to your Personal Address List, but the dialog box looks the same (see Figure 16.1).

ADDING NEW ENTRIES TO THE PERSONAL ADDRESS BOOK

To add a completely new address to your Personal Address Book, follow these steps:

1. Choose Tools, Address Book or click the Address Book tool button on the toolbar. The Address Book dialog box appears (refer to Figure 16.1).

2. Click the New Entry button or choose File, New Entry. The New Entry dialog box appears (see Figure 16.2).

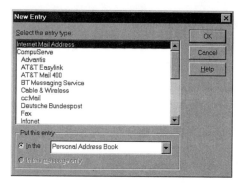

FIGURE 16.2   Choose a source for your new entry.

3. In the Select The Entry Type list, choose from the available options, and then click OK. Additionally, you can choose to add one of the following two items:

   • Personal Distribution List   Use this to create one address entry for a group of recipients. When you send mail to the list name, everyone on the list receives the message. You might use this option for grouping department heads, for example.

   • Other Address   Choose this option to add one new recipient at a time. You can enter a name, e-mail address, and e-mail type for each entry. In addition, you can enter business addresses and phone numbers, and you can add notes and comments to the entry. Use this entry for Internet addresses, for example.

4. A dialog box appears in which you fill in the information about the person. The dialog box tabs depend on what

type you chose in step 3, but in general, the tab where you put the required information appears on top (for example, SMTP—Internet in Figure 16.3) and optional tabs appear behind it. Enter the required information, and extra information if desired, and then click OK.

 SMTP   Stands for Simple Mail Transport Protocol. A communication protocol standard for exchanging e-mail between Internet hosts.

5. When you're done working in your Personal Address Book, close the Address Book window. You're returned to the Outlook Inbox.

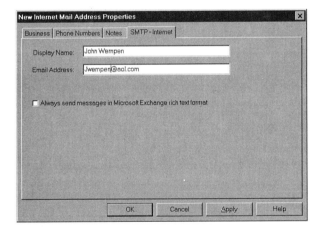

FIGURE 16.3   Outlook displays the tab containing the required information first. You can choose the other tabs if you want.

VIEWING THE LIST OF ADDRESSES

The following points outline some of the ways in which you might use the Address List:

- To view more details about any entry in the Address Book dialog box, double-click the person's name or click the Properties button on the toolbar. The person's Properties dialog box appears, with her name, address type, postoffice name, and network type listed on the Address (1) tab.

- Click the Properties toolbar button and choose the Address (2) tab in the person's Properties dialog box to view her phone number, office, or department, and any notes or comments that have been added to the description.

- If you cannot find a particular name in the list, you can search for it. Choose Tools, Find or click the Find button, and then enter the name for which you're searching in the Find Name Beginning With text box. Click OK to start the search.

Click OK to close the dialog box and return to the Address Book dialog box.

SENDING A MESSAGE TO SOMEONE IN THE ADDRESS BOOK

You can use either of the address books to choose the names of recipients to whom you want to send new messages, forward messages, or send a reply. Using the address books also makes sending carbon copies and blind carbon copies easy.

 Blind Carbon Copy A blind carbon copy (Bcc) of a message is a copy that's sent to someone in secret; the other recipients have no way of knowing that you're sending the message to someone via a blind carbon copy. By the same token, you have no way of knowing whether the e-mail you receive was sent to another person.

To address a message, follow these steps:

1. Choose Compose, New Mail Message from the Outlook Inbox window, or click the New Mail Message toolbar button.

2. In the Message window, click the To button to display the Select Names dialog box.

3. Open Show Names from the drop-down list box and choose either the Postoffice Address List or the Personal Address Book.

4. From the list that appears on the left, choose the name of the intended recipient and select the To button. Outlook copies the name to the Message Recipients list. You can add multiple names if you want.

5. (Optional) Select the names of anyone to whom you want to send a carbon copy and click the Cc button to transfer those names to the Message Recipients list.

6. (Optional) Select the names of anyone to whom you want to send a blind carbon copy and click the Bcc button. Figure 16.4 shows two recipients for a message plus two more people to receive blind carbon copies.

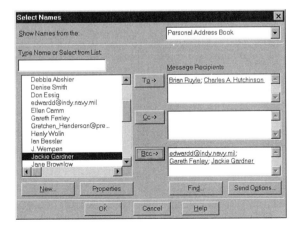

FIGURE 16.4   Choose the recipients from this listing.

7. Click OK to return to the Message window and complete your message.

CREATING A NEW CONTACT

In Outlook, a contact is any person or company for which you've entered a name, address, phone number, or other information. You can communicate with a contact in Outlook by sending an e-mail message, scheduling a meeting, or sending a letter.

You use the Contacts folder to create, store, and utilize your Contacts list. You also can edit the information at any time, add new contacts, or delete contacts from the list. To create a new contact, follow these steps:

1. Click the Contacts folder or open the Folder List and choose Contacts. If you haven't used the list before, the folder is empty.

2. Choose Contacts, New Contact, or click the New Contact button on the Toolbar. The Contact dialog box appears, with the General tab displayed (see Figure 16.5).

3. Click the Full Name button to display the Check Full Name dialog box, and then enter the contact's title and full name (including first, middle, and last names) and any suffix you want to include. Alternatively, you can type the name directly in the text box.

4. (Optional) Enter the client's company name and job title.

5. In the File As drop-down box, enter or select the method by which you want to file your contact's names. You can choose last name first or first name first, or you can enter your own filing system, such as by company or state.

6. (Optional) Enter the address in the Address box and choose whether the address is Business, Home, or Other. Alternatively, you can click the Address button to enter the street, city, state, zip code, and country in specified areas instead of all within the text block. You can add a second address (say, the Home address) if you want.

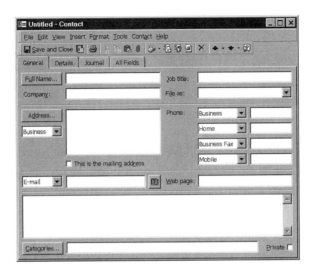

FIGURE 16.5 You can enter as much or as little information about each contact as you need.

7. In the Phone drop-down lists, choose the type of phone number—Business, Callback, Car, Home Fax, ISDN, or Pager—and then enter the number. You can enter up to 19 numbers in each of the four drop-down boxes in the Phone area of the dialog box.

8. (Optional) Enter up to three e-mail addresses in the E-mail text box. In the Web Page text box, enter the address for the company or contact's Web page on the Internet.

9. (Optional) In the comment text box, enter any descriptions, comments, or other pertinent information you want. Then select or enter a category to classify the contact. You may choose from a variety of categories. Simply check the box next to the desired category.

10. Open the File menu and choose Save to save the record and close the Contact dialog box.

You can edit the information about a contact at any time by double-clicking the contact's name in the Contacts list; this displays the contact's information window. Alternatively, you can click within the information listed below a contact's name (such as the phone number or address) to position the insertion point in the text, and then delete or enter text. Press Enter to complete the modifications you've made and move to the next contact in the list.

VIEWING THE CONTACTS LIST

By default, you see the contacts in an Address Cards view. The information you see is the contact's name and other data such as addresses and phone numbers. The contact's company name, job title, and comments, however, are not displayed by default. Figure 16.6 shows the Contacts list in the default Address Cards view.

You can use the horizontal scroll bar to view more contacts, or you can click a letter in the index to display contacts beginning with that letter in the first column of the list.

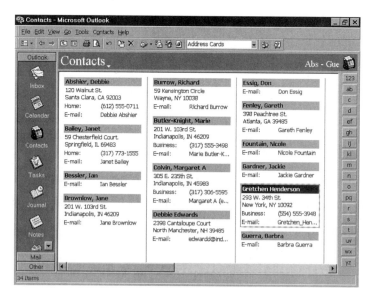

FIGURE 16.6   View your contacts in Address Cards view.

You can change how you view the contacts in the list by choosing one of these options from the Current View drop-down list on the standard toolbar:

- Address Cards   Displays File As names (last name first and first name last), addresses, and phone numbers of the contacts, depending on the amount of information you've entered in a card format.

- Detailed Address Cards   Displays File As name, full name, job title, company, addresses, phone numbers, e-mail addresses, categories, and comments in a card format.

- Phone List   Displays full name, job title, company, File As name, department, phone numbers, and categories in a table, organizing each entry horizontally in rows and columns.

- By Category   Displays contacts in rows by categories. The information displayed is the same as what's displayed in a phone list.

- By Company   Displays contacts in rows, grouped by their company. The information displayed is the same as what's displayed in a phone list.

- By Location   Displays contacts grouped by country. The information displayed is the same as what's displayed in a phone list.

COMMUNICATING WITH A CONTACT

You can send messages to any of your contacts, arrange meetings, assign tasks, or even send a letter to a contact from within Outlook. To communicate with a contact, make sure you're in the Contacts folder. You do not need to open the specific contact's information window to perform any of the following procedures.

Sending a Message to a Contact

To send a message from the Contacts folder, select the contact and choose Contacts, New Message To Contact or click the New Message To Contact button. In the Untitled—Message dialog box, enter the subject and message and set any options you want. When you're ready to send the message, click the Send button.

To send a message to a contact, you must make sure you've entered an e-mail address in the General tab of the Contact dialog box for that particular contact. If Outlook cannot locate the mailing address, it displays the message dialog box shown in Figure 16.7.

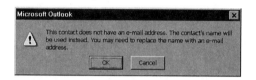

Figure 16.7   Outlook cannot send the message until you complete the address in the New Message dialog box.

Scheduling with a Contact

To schedule a meeting with a contact, the contact must have a valid e-mail address. If no address is listed for the contact, Outlook notifies you with a message box and enables you to enter an address within the Message dialog box. If the listed address is not found, Outlook responds with the Check Names dialog box.

To schedule a meeting with a contact, select the contact and choose Contacts, New Meeting With Contact or click the New Meeting With Contact button. The Untitled—Meeting dialog box appears. Enter the subject, location, time and date, and other information you need to schedule the meeting, and then notify the contact by sending an invitation.

ASSIGNING TASKS TO A CONTACT

Tasks are assigned through e-mail. Therefore, you must enter a valid e-mail address for the contact before you can assign him or her a task.

To assign a task to a contact, select the contact and choose Contacts, New Task For Contact. The Task dialog box appears. Enter the subject, due date, status, and other information, and then send the task to the contact.

SENDING A LETTER TO A CONTACT

Outlook uses the Microsoft Word Letter Wizard to help you create a letter to send to a contact. Within the Word Wizard, follow the directions as they appear onscreen to complete the text of the letter.

To send a letter to the contact, select the contact in the Contact folder and choose Contacts, New Letter To Contact. Word opens the Letter Wizard on-screen. The Letter Wizard helps you format and complete the letter. You can click the Office Assistant button if you need additional help. Then all you have to do is follow the directions and make your choices.

In this lesson, you learned to use Outlook's Address Book with your e-mail and create and work with a contacts list.

INDEX

selecting (Word documents),
9-10
special effects (Word documents), 11
Format menu commands, *see*
commands
Format Painter (Excel worksheets),
80
formatting
Excel worksheets
AutoFormat, 78-79
conditional formatting, 80
*Format Painter (copying
formats), 80*
number formats, 68-71
text, 71-78
table fields, 123
text
*composing email (Outlook),
188-189*
spell checking, 189-192
Word documents
styles, 44-50
templates, 50-54
Formatting toolbar (Word), 10
forms, database (Access), 101-102
formulas (Excel 97 worksheets),
see **Excel 97 worksheets**
forwarding email (Outlook),
183-184
**Function Wizard (Excel worksheet
functions), 96-97**
functions (Excel 97 worksheets),
91-97

G-H

grammar checker (Word), 28-30
graphical user interfaces, *see* **GUIs**
graphics (presentations), 156, 167
GUIs (graphical user interface), 1

Hyperlink data type (table fields),
123
hyperlinks (presentations), 170,
172

I

IF function (Excel), 92
Import Table Wizard (Access), 116
indentations (Word documents),
14-16
Insert menu commands, *see*
commands
inserting
cells (Excel worksheets), 62-63
columns (Excel worksheets),
65-66
rows (Excel worksheets), 65-66
tables into Word documents,
38-43
WordArt into slides, 167-168
italics, applying to fonts (Word),
10

J-L

justification (Word documents),
16

line breaks (Word documents),
19-21
Link Table Wizard (Access), 116
lists (presentations), 166
**Lookup Wizard data type (table
fields), 123**

M

margin settings (printing), 6
Match Case search option, 26
**mathematical operators (Excel
worksheet formulas), 83-84**
MAX function (Excel), 93
Memo data type (table fields), 123
merging cells (Excel worksheets),
63-65
**messages, email (Outlook), 187-
200**
Microsoft Access, *see* **Access**
MIN function (Excel), 93